WILD RIDE TO DEMOCRACY

WILD RIDE TO DEMOCRACY

Dr. Bob Spear

Printed in the United States of America
ISBN 978-1-7330976-8-0

Author's Contact info:
Email: bob_spear@hotmail.com
Illustrations by ChatGPT, Canva AI, and Microsoft Co-Pilot, modified by the author

21CommonSense LLC
190 South Shore Road
Swanton, Maryland 21561, USA

DEDICATION

This book is dedicated to

MOUNTAIN MARYLAND VOICES,

My friends and neighbors in

Garrett and Allegany Counties,

Always Smiling Advocates

For Freedom and Democracy

Table of Contents

WILD RIDE TO DEMOCRACY

RADICAL REFORM

"Desperate times call for desperate measures."

We now have a five-alarm fire. We need radical reform measures to rescue American democracy; half-measures and a piecemeal approach will no longer work.

We need leaders who will return us to a democracy based on a revised Constitution II. Such leaders will convene the Constitution II Convention, supervise the ratification process, and transition to the new Constitution. Our mission in this short book is to define the necessary reforms and how to realize them,

Need for a System Reset

OUR HAPPY PLANS

This guide for the establishment of a happy democracy in the United States is based on the ideals and structures of the original

1787 Constitution as amended, while also improving and modernizing those structures. Commentary elucidates the rationale, explains new procedures, and also suggests a method of implementation.

In recent years, but most especially during the Trump presidencies, we have strayed egregiously from our original ideals and constitutional norms, our love for each other, our patriotism. Here is a roadmap back to sanity, to democracy, to our ideals.

UNDERPINNINGS

Before we get to a discussion of democracy and of an improved American future, we should agree on some fundamentals – the underpinnings which make a discussion of democracy apropos of our current condition. We should agree, or largely agree, on our core values, philosophy, ideology, economic system, and type of government. I summarize here my own views on these topics, and trust that you will concur.

Underpinnings of Democracy

CORE VALUES

As I campaigned (unsuccessfully) for the Maryland House of Delegates in Ruby Red western Maryland in 2022, I was constantly struck by the common beliefs of nearly all my constituents, regardless of political affiliation. We all need and want the basic necessities of life: food, clothing, shelter. We all want safety from bad guys at home (criminals) and bad guys abroad (hostile foreign powers). We all want protection and recovery from man-made and natural disasters. We all want medical care, safe food, childcare, education, public infrastructure, eldercare, support for veterans, and a better future for our children.

Finding Common Ground

Among friends who agree on these core values, we sometimes disagree on how best to achieve them and on the extent to which government should be relied on to help. But that is the stuff of policies and politics, where people with a common set of core values can debate alternative solutions to problems. Politics do not alter our core values.

TRUTH

One of the most important core values most of us hold dear is TRUTH, without which no meaningful political discussion can take place. Yet TRUTH appears to have become collateral damage in our current political wars, and this is something we need to fix if we are ever to find our way forward out of this morass. Here are a few suggestions:

- Expect ALL to speak TRUTH. Do not tolerate LIES. We must all be held accountable if we lie about a stolen election, about unproven election fraud, or about an opponent's record, qualifications, or statements.
- When it comes to libel, treat Facebook, Twitter, Instagram, TikTok, and other social media platforms more like newspapers and less like telephones. Hold them accountable for lies. Hold them accountable for content that appears on their platforms and reaches more than five people.

Speak TRUTH! Avoid LIES!

- Let's reset the standard for defamation: we must hold people accountable for the things they say in public. Allow victims, even "public persons", to successfully sue for libel. The only defense against such a lawsuit is a demonstration that the attack was truthful.
- Require broadcasters to fairly treat both sides (that is, reimpose the Fairness Doctrine).

OPTIMISTIC PHILOSOPHY

FDR Campaign (1932)

Happy Days Are Here Again[1]

I cannot imagine that my philosophy of life differs much from that of most Americans, though admittedly we do have a few negative folks among us. I am largely optimistic toward life and believe we can improve the human condition, cure disease, eradicate poverty and homelessness, and make a better life for all. I believe in science, and I believe that a solid public education system is like a rising tide, lifting all boats. I care for my fellow man, especially those less fortunate than myself.

---

[1] https://soundbeat.org/episode/happy-days-are-here-again/ Image: FDR with Anna Roosevelt Halsted and Eleanor Roosevelt during campaign at Warm Springs, Georgia, October 24, 1932. Licensed under the terms of the cc-by-2.0.

Optimistic Philosophy

This country's success was built on the labor of American and immigrant workers, as well as entrepreneurship and invention. The people at the top of the economic order work as hard as those less fortunate, but they also benefit from inherited wealth, racial and social biases, and good fortune. The claims of people at the top that those at the bottom are lazy are simply not factual (most working class people work hard, often holding two or three jobs while raising families and still struggling to make ends meet). The claims of people at the bottom that those at the top are lazy and just lucky are not factual either, as many of the wealthy also work hard, take risks, save their money, and invest wisely – though some have fallen into their wealth through no fault of their own,

Reprising the French Revolution

Vast inequalities between social classes are a significant societal threat, and we should work to reduce such inequalities and raise the middle class. Even people at the top should recognize that a large, angry underclass is unhealthy for themselves and for the whole of society. Think of the class inequalities that led to the French Revolution. As one of the super-rich zillionaires once remarked, "They'll be coming for us with pitchforks."

AMERICAN IDEOLOGY

I wholeheartedly embrace the ideals in the 1776 Declaration of Independence, that every person is created equal, endowed with inalienable rights to life, liberty, and the pursuit of happiness. I believe in the 1948 Universal Declaration of Rights, that each human is equal and should be treated fairly without regard to race, sex, ethnicity, religion, heritage, or geography. In agreement with Pope Leo XIII's famous encyclical "Rerum Novarum" (1891), I believe in the value of labor, the right of workers to organize, and the obligation of management to work for the amelioration of poverty. I believe in democracy, in majority rule, and in "one man, one vote."

American Ideology

In the United States, we have a long history of maltreatment of the less fortunate, the poor, the sick, and racial and ethnic minorities. Hence, in modern practice, this means that Diversity, Equity, and Inclusion (DEI) represent societal norms that should be valued, not disparaged. "Diversity" recognizes that America is made up of diverse peoples in every sense of that word – people from every race, creed, nation, background, and identity. "Inclusion" means that we strive to include all of this diversity in every aspect of our communal life. And "equity" means that everyone is afforded equality of opportunity – not equal outcomes, but an equal shot at getting there.

LIMITED CAPITALISM

The world has experienced a panoply of economic systems, including capitalism, fascism, socialism, communism, mercantilism, tribalism, individualism, libertarianism, and so on and so on. These systems all come down to three central questions:1) To what extent is each individual able to determine his own economic destiny? 2) How much of our economy is a joint, communal enterprise? and 3) Who gets to call the shots?

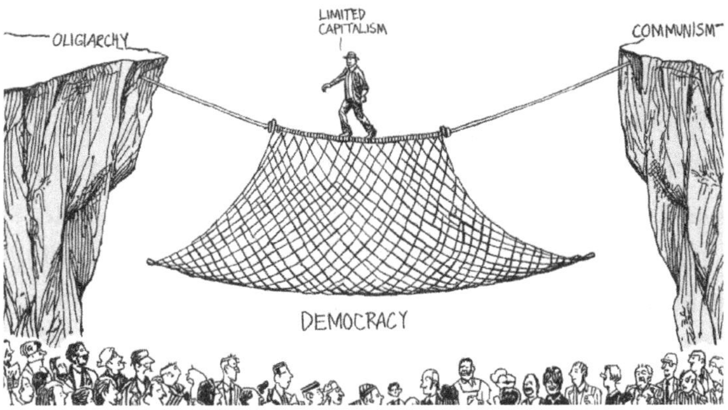

Limited Capitalism, with Democracy as the Social Safety Net

In the United States, our chosen economic system is one of limited capitalism, in which free enterprise is encouraged to flourish, but capitalism's inherent excesses are curtailed, and a social safety net protects the most vulnerable. We do not want unbridled wealth, monopolies, and the oligarchy that inevitably results; nor do we want communism and the elimination of private enterprise. Where and how to draw the line between these extremes is a matter for constant debate and adjustment. Again, we can argue around the edges, but most of us generally agree that limited capitalism fits us best. The notion of competing interests between management and labor is just as healthy as the inherent conflict between prosecution and defense in a courtroom.

WE CHOOSE REPRESENTATIVE DEMOCRACY

Representative Democracy

What form of government supports our core values, philosophy, ideology, and economy? Human societies have experimented with multiple models, including one-man rule (monarchy, dictatorship, autocracy), few-over-many (aristocracy, oligarchy, mafia-style cabal), proletariat over all (communist), and republic (bottom-up rather than top-down, representative democracy at its best). Someone once wrote, "Peoples get the governments they deserve." Do we deserve a republic? When asked by an onlooker at the end of the Constitutional Convention of 1787 whether the delegates had given us a monarchy or a republic, Ben Franklin famously answered, "A republic, if you can keep it!"

Hence, I do believe, as do most Americans, that a representative democracy fits America best. Perhaps democracy IS best. I believe, as Winston Churchill once remarked, "Democracy is the worst possible form of government, except for all other possible forms of government!".

Three Pillars of Democracy

And what are the three pillars that operationalize representative democracy? 1) majority rule at every level, from voting to the highest officials, 2) limited government, meaning that a majority of voters empower the government to do some things and nothing else, and 3) BELIEF in democracy by the society writ large.

Polls consistently show that a strong majority of Americans still believe that democracy is the best form of government and that it is right for us. 78% (in a 2022 poll) favored democracy over dictatorship, and only 9% preferred a dictatorship. Three quarters agree that democracy, despite its problems, is still the bast form of government. Most Americans associate democracy with our foundational political values of fair elections, freedom of speech, civil rights, and civil liberties.

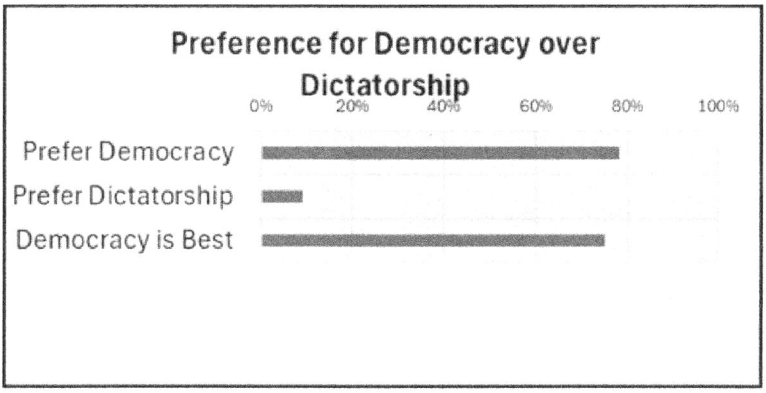

A CONTRARY VIEW

We must recognize that a significant minority of the American population disagrees with everything I have written so far and have done so for the duration of the American Federation. We need to recognize that this contrary view exists before rejecting it.

In his landmark 2012 book *American Nations* and subsequent *Nations Apart*, Colin Woodard[2] describes the 11 nations that settled North America and left their cultural footprints on specific swaths of the continent. The boundaries of these 11 nations do not follow state or provincial or international borders. In the United States, over multiple generations, coalitions of these nations have squared off against each other in endless arguments about democracy, about what it means to be an American, about states' rights, about the proper role of the Federal Government, about gerrymandering and voting rights, and about policies concerning abortion, gun control, taxpayer-supported medical care, the social safety net, education, campaign financing, the free press, immigration, separation of church and state, organized labor, income disparity, and war and peace – among others.

---

[2] Woodard, Colin. *American Nations: A History of the Eleven Rival Regional Cultures of North America* (2012). Penguin Books. AND Woodard, Colin. *Nations Apart: How Clashing Regional Cultures Shattered America* (2025). Viking.

3

In Woodard's characterizations, the current coalition of Yankeedom, the Midlands, New Netherlands, and the Left Coast (roughly the Blue states that these nations control) support universal voting, universal medical care, a robust social safety net, Federal funding of science, health and food and drug safety, limits on campaign financing, free and well-funded public education, abortion and other reproductive rights, unions, libraries, raising taxes on wealthy individuals and corporations, public financing of election campaigns, Congressional oversight of the Executive Branch, protection of the environment, gun control, foreign aid, immigrant rights, and gun control – among other issues. Essentially, this coalition views Government as efficacious and an effective partner with citizens and states in the achievement of communal objectives. Government has a leading role in helping society become more fair by emphasizing diversity, equity, and inclusion (DEI). This coalition opts for liberal democracy in its traditional sense.

---

[3] Woodard, Colin. *American Nations, op. cit.* Usef with permission,

An opposing coalition of the Deep South, Greater Appalachia, New France, and the Far West (roughly the Red states) argues against all of these initiatives and instead campaigns for reduced taxes on the wealthy and corporations, limitless campaign contributions, a return to the imaginary (fake) always-glorious American history taught in the 1950's, reduced support for public education, political litmus tests for support of science research, no foreign aid, severe restrictions on immigration, reductions on the reach of the social safety net, elimination of reproductive rights, voter suppression (making sure only the "right people" vote), free enterprise, *laissez-faire* economics, book banning, and reimposition of the racial caste system that obtained prior to the Civil Rights Movement. Some even want to take away the right of women to vote and birthright citizenship. Needless to say, they oppose all DEI programs. This coalition views Government as The Problem and wants to do away with it as far as possible. Rejecting Congressional interference with the Executive, it favors the Imperial Presidency. This coalition represents illiberalism at its worst; proponents fundamentally fear democracy.

One can debate which coalition has the better philosophical argument, but you cannot really argue with the factual outcomes. Collectively, the Blue states outperform the Red states in just about every measure one can think of, from educational attainment, to income and wealth, to longevity, to health, to crime rates, to happiness.

In my reading of American social and political history, it seems to me that these coalitions, or some versions of them, have been arguing about fundamental issues of our political system forever. It also seems apparent to me that the liberal side has been fighting against a stacked deck for way too long. The existing political system is rigged in favor of the conservative, Republican minority, and it is time to change it. The rules of the system preclude meaningful change from within the system, and so it becomes necessary to initiate change from outside the system, while preserving as much of the current system, (that is, the fair parts) as is possible without violating the core principles of democracy. This book presents a peaceful revolution in the way the American system of government works.

CONCLUSION

The 1787 Constitution introduced a new and untried republican form of government, a representative democracy, with lots of caveats and compromises and insufficiencies. Recent Supreme Court decisions and an autocratic president have eviscerated our Constitution, and Congress has chosen to stand by and watch. Therefore, the time is ripe for a constitutional do-over. And the Supreme Court has given us leave to do precisely that.

WHAT'S WRONG?

The original Framers and succeeding generations of Americans have been attempting to perfect our imperfect democracy for 250 years. In a truly representative democracy, the citizens

- Reach a consensus on the philosophical framework of the government; that is, the citizens adopt a government that reflects their core values.
- Ratify the constitution, which creates specific governmental structures and broadly outlines government functions.

- Select representatives who act in accordance with the constitution to create, execute, and enforce laws that carry out the functions specified in the constitution.

While we claim to be a democracy, in practice our democratic structures are weak and ineffective at best, anti-democratic at worst. Everyone knows this. It's high time that we take resolute action to fix it.

What's Wrong?

Among the Framers most brilliant devices for maintaining democracy is the separation of powers: The Federal Government has limited powers, leaving many aspects of daily life to the states and to the people. Within the Federal Government, power is divided among three co-equal branches: Article I of the Constitution gives all legislative power to Congress; Article II gives all executive power to the President; and Article III gives all judicial power to the Supreme Court and such other inferior courts as Congress may establish. Each branch operates within its own sphere, and a careful system of checks and balances inhibits each branch from encroaching on the powers of the other two, while also allowing each branch to exercise restraint over the unbridled power of the other two. Over the years, Congress has also chosen to limit the power of the Executive Branch by creating a series of quasi-independent agencies, such as the Federal Reserve Bank, the FBI, the Federal Communications Commission, and the Federal Elections Commission.

This piece, the checks and balances, might be the piece of our government which is most broken. Over the last century, Congress has ceded most of its real power to the Executive, and what little remains, Donald Trump is attempting to grab for himself. The President now uses Executive Orders (mentioned nowhere in the Constitution) whenever he wants to do something that has not been authorized by Congress. President Trump has refused to spend money for programs mandated by law, and he orders expenditures that have not been authorized. He tries every day to destroy the independence of the agencies specifically designed by Congress to be independent. He has initiated many Executive Orders that challenge free speech (1st Amendment), warrantless search and seizure (4th Amendment}, and birthright citizenship (14th Amendment). He initiates vindictive lawsuits against anyone and everyone he perceives to be his enemy. Meanwhile, the Supreme Court has failed to protect the separation of powers built into the Constitution or to prevent Executive overreach. Over and over again, the Court has sided with the Executive, giving him *carte blanche* to do whatever he pleases.

Checks and balances, unchecked and unbalanced

A principal reason for Congress's failure to restrain the Executive is that Congress itself is anti-democratic. The U.S. Senate was designed to represent states rather than people, and even when the Supreme Court decided that "one man, one vote" should be the rule of the land, it did not apply that democratic standard to the makeup of the Senate. In addition, rampant gerrymandering of Congressional Districts (as well as state legislative districts) has left us with a Congress which in no way represents the people.

Our democracy falls short of the ideal in its inherent anti-democratic structures. We need a Constitution ratified by the people, national leaders (president and vice president) selected by all the people, a Congress that represents its constituents, fair elections, meaningful separation of powers, and a judiciary that enforces the Constitution's limits.

While we still believe in democracy conceptually, we are largely unsatisfied with how our American democracy is currently working. Recent polls show that only 28% of us say that our democracy is a model for the world; 34% are satisfied with how our democracy is working; 30% believe that our current political divisions are not a threat to democracy; and only 22% trust that the government will do the right thing all or most of the time.

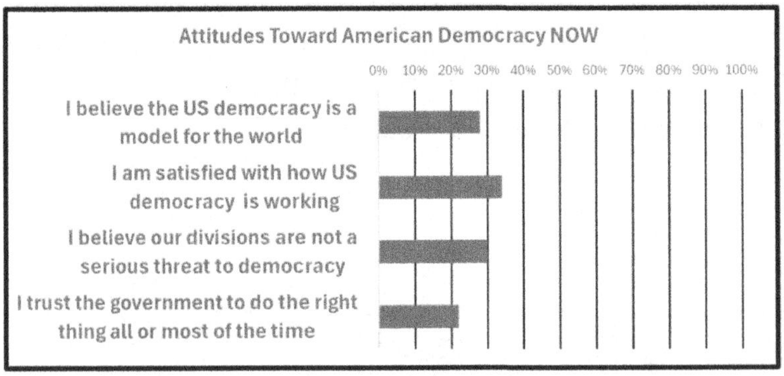

People often complain that both major political parties have failed to deliver the government that the majority of citizens desire. This is obviously the case during successive man-made disasters of the last decades, from free trade to the Iraq War, to the financial meltdown of 2007, to the housing and mortgage failures, to the opioid crisis, to crime, to the collapse of soybean farms. Both parties have failed to address the real concerns of the American people, while none of those responsible for these failures have gone to jail. Instead, we just give tax breaks to folks who don't need them.

But in my view, the problem is less in bad policies and inept leaders and more in the underlying system. Systematic political reform – making our government actually democratic – would give us a much better chance of implementing the policies the populace demands. Yet, as we have seen for many years, the anti-democratic characteristics of our system prevent any meaningful change.

ELEMENTS OF THE FIX

Elements of a Fix

We must incorporate the principles of democracy into our Constitution. Specifically, we must adopt majority rule wherever possible, we must ensure that our rights are preserved, and we must strengthen the checks and balances which operationalize the concept of limited government. We must then select public officials who are committed to democracy and to carrying out the principles of democracy as embodied in the Constitution. And then we must hold them accountable for doing so.

Remember our Three Pillars of Democracy:

- Majority Rule – the Fix must follow majority rule in all decision-making.
- Limited Government – meaning that the Government can do only certain things and nothing else, and meaning also that an effective system of checks and balances prevents any part of the Government from getting out of control.
- Belief in Democracy – meaning that officials and citizens need to believe in our system, and meaning also that the structures we adopt encourage citizens to have faith in that system.

Here is a brief list of the new elements of democracy which we need to adopt:

Ihe Constitution belongs to the voters.
And only they can amend it.

- Voter approval of the Constitution and any future amendments. At present, voters do not and did not adopt the original Constitution, and voters have no role in proposing or ratifying amendments to the Constitution. These powers are given to Congress and to state legislatures. But in 49 of the 50 states (Delaware is the exception), voters must approve amendments to the state constitution. The same should obtain at the Federal level.

- Direct election of the President. At present, the Electoral College elects the President, and the Electoral College unfairly favors states with small populations. You may think that you vote for a presidential candidate, but in reality you vote for an elector to the Electoral College.

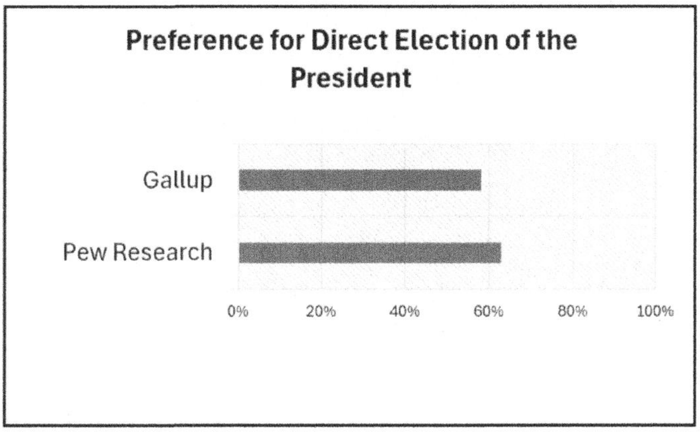

Most Americans prefer the direct election of the president rather than the current Electoral College System (polls taken in September 2024).

- Direct (separate) election of the Vice President, renamed as Chancellor of the Senate. At present, you vote for a presidential and vice-presidential candidate, combined into one ticket. In modern practice, the presidential candidate alone selects the vice-presidential candidate.
- A representative Senate, with Senatorial Districts based on the population of each state. At present, each state elects two Senators, regardless of population. This is hardly fair. A voter in Wyoming has 69 times as much power to choose a Senator as a voter in California and 40 times as much power as a voter in Texas. We need to implement the "one man, one vote" rule for electing the Senate. At present, a Wyoming or Montana or North Dakota constituent has a vastly better chance of meeting with and influencing their Senator compared to a resident of California or Texas. At the same time, we do want to maintain some continuity with the existing Seante – longer terms than the House, staggered elections, some manner of representation for the state, and the Senate's advise-and-consent role on treaties and on presidential and judicial appointments.
- A representative House, with a much smaller population in each Congressional District (CD). At present, each House

member represents about 730,000 people. Many Americans cannot name their Representative, and few have ever met them. For the "People's House", this is not healthy. Let's reduce the number of people represented by each House member to a half million, which will make the House much more responsive to the people but arguably still not too large as to be unwieldy – it would have about 700 members, and it would grow proportionally as the US population grows. By the way, according to the 1787 Constitution, each House member in the first Congress represented no more than 30,000 people; and when the current permanent House size of 435 members was adopted in 1929, the average CD had 277,000 people. Therefore, even a half million per member might be too many constituents. If we went back to the 277,000 per member that obtained in 1929, the House would have about 1200 members; and if we returned to the 30,000 per House member we had in the first Congress, the House would have a whopping 11,000 members!

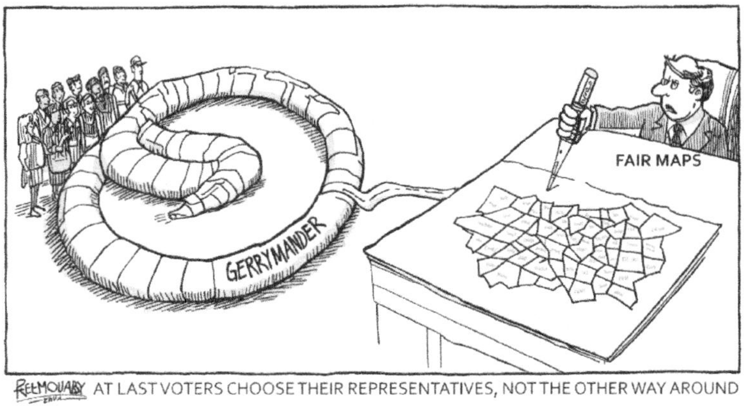

End Gerrymandering

- An end to gerrymandering for all elected offices – House, Senate, and state legislative districts. At present, many states are severely gerrymandered, resulting in very unfair representation in Congress.

Open Primaries & RCV

- Open primaries, with Ranked Choice Voting determining the three candidates who qualify for the general election. At present, voting in many primaries is limited to voters from the same political party as the candidate, and voters are not able to choose candidates from different parties for different offices. Further, in many states, independent voters cannot vote in any primary.
- Ranked Choice Voting to determine the winner of each general election

Universal Suffrage – the cornerstone of a true democracy."

Universal Suffrage & Compulsory Voting

- Universal suffrage for all citizens age 18+; compulsory voting; and voting by multiple means: in-person, by mail, and online (if online voting can be made secure).

Fundamental Rights

- Specification of the rights of all people and of all citizens – that is, a new Bill of Rights.

Chancellor Appointing a Supreme court Justice

- A newly reconstituted Federal judiciary, with 16-year terms of office, and with appointment of judges by the Chancellor instead of the President.

"PROTECTING THOSE WHO SERVE THE PUBLIC – NOT THE POWERFUL."

Civil Servants

- Protection for civil servants, for Congressional mandates, and for independent agencies

"Checks and Balances - Every Order Needs the People's Stamp."

- Congressional veto power over all Executive Orders

Separation of Powers – The Strength of Democracy.

- Re-enforcement of the separation of powers, and redefinition of the relative powers of Congress, the President, and the states.

A Constitutional Court Accountable to All

- A Constitutional Court that enforces the Constitution and is accountable to the public.

ADOPTION OF THE FIX

Let's be radical, while also being generous. Barcelona's most famous architect Antonin Gaudi advised: "To do anything, first you need love, then technique." Therefore, we need to work for a solution based on love of our countrymen, based also on their input and their approval and advice. I suggest the following platform for the re-establishment of constitutional representative democracy in the United States.

We do not need to worry about implementing fixes which some might consider unconstitutional, nor do we need to worry about amending the Constitution using a procedure not specified in the 1787 Constitution. This is true for two reasons:

Articles of Confederation vs 1787 Constitution

1. We have the precedent of the 1787 Constitution itself. The Articles of Confederation, adopted by the 13 original states in 1781, specified that any amendments to the Articles of Confederation must be agreed to unanimously by the legislature of each of those 13 states. But the delegates to the 1787 Constitutional Convention knew that several states would refuse to ratify any significant changes to the Articles of Confederation. Therefore, the delegates agreed to simply ignore the procedure for legally amending the Articles of

Confederation. Rather, they adopted a totally new form of government and invited all 13 states to approve it. They also specified that this new Constitution would come into effect when ¾ of the states (that is, 9 states) had approved it. This scheme worked. When 9 states ratified the new Constitution, the current United States was born. (The remaining states came along in due course.) So today we can use the same principle, based on historical precedent.

Destruction of the Constitution

2. The Supreme Court and the Trump Administration have already trashed the Constitution beyond any reasonable facsimile to the original document. To wit:
    a. In 2024, the Supreme Court decided that a President can do anything they want with impunity. This means that a President cannot be held accountable for anything they do or try to do.
    b. Also in 2024, the Supreme Court ignored the provision of the 14th Amendment which precludes from holding public office anyone who has engaged in insurrection against the United States, which Trump and his MAGA cabal did on January 6, 2021.
    c. Trump unilaterally imposed tariffs on goods imported into the United States, despite his lack of authority to

do so. The power to impose tariffs ("duties" in the words of the Constitution) rests solely with Congress. Trump has also cancelled programs, closed agencies, and fired thousands of Federal workers without any justification and without any legal authority. And to a large extent, Congress and the Courts have permitted him to do so.

d. Trump is attempting to implement his mass deportation scheme using illegal ICE raids and ignoring Constitutional protections for immigrants and citizens alike. Hi approach includes violent suppression of protests, warrantless searches and seizures, attacks on the free press, illegal use of the military for domestic purposes, and concentration camps. He has vastly expanded his army of faceless armed thugs, similar to the Nazi SA (Brown Shirts) and SS (Black Shirts) of the 1930's.

e. Trump is trying to take over Constitutionally-protected powers of state governments, especially voting. He attacks dissent in every form, but especially from governors of Blue states.

f. One of the Supreme Court's most anti-democratic decisions occurred in 2010, when the Court ruled in the *Citizens United* case that most limits on corporate campaign contributions are unconstitutional. This decision opened the floodgates to dark money dominating our politics. Spending money to influence politicians is a form of free speech, said the Court, and corporations have free speech rights just like people. This contorted decision ignored the fact that billionaires and billionaire corporations can afford a lot more free speech than Joe Citizen, not exactly an even playing field. Some analysts conclude that the *Citizens United* decision alone explains a whole lot about what ails our dysfunctional political system.

g. For two centuries, Congress debated, defeated, and passed many bills designed to limit the personal possession of firearms, and it was widely accepted

> that Congress had the authority to do this. The clear, plain-language of the Second Amendment only protects the right of each state to maintain a militia, which necessarily includes the possession of firearms when serving in that capacity. But in the Heller decision in 2008, the Supreme Court decided to ignore the state militia clause and instead decided that every citizen has a right to possess a firearm. Every citizen's right to life is not so protected, and after the Heller decision, every legislative effort to protect life by restricting firearms possession has been declared unconstitutional.

In sum, a new President has no obligation to follow the Constitution either.

Again, let me emphasize that these failures of democracy are larger than any one President or Supreme Court. The so-called "Imperial Presidency" has evolved over many decades, with little public concern, abrogation of powers by Congress, and a wink and a nod (if not outright collusion) from the judiciary. Hence, replacing Trump and/or the current justices and/or our current elected representatives will not fix the problem – that may give us a temporary respite but will just leave us open to another autocrat next time. Rather, we need to fix the underlying systemic issues.

Accordingly, new American leaders have the power to immediately take whatever action they deem necessary to reestablish constitutional democracy, including closing the Supreme Court and suspending Congress pending new elections under a fair system of representation. We do not need to only defeat Trumpism, if we are then left with a severely weakened democracy open to abuse by any future government of any political party. Instead, we need a total system reset.

The reset can and should be accomplished without resort to violence, at least on the part of those seeking change. Those trying to prevent change may employ violence, but the peaceful majority of Americans have strength in numbers and will win out in the end.

We need two things to fix the mess we find ourselves in: (1) willing leaders with widespread support from the citizenry and (2) a Radical Action Plan (RAP) that outlines the necessary steps. Let me discuss Leadership first, followed by the suggested RAP that these leaders should follow.

LEADERSHIP

Implementation of a total system reset requires leadership willing and able to do it. I see four possible scenarios leading to this outcome; vocal citizen engagement is mandatory for any of the four to work. I describe these four scenarios here in order from easiest to hardest of realization.

Presidential Scenario.

The easiest and most straightforward scenario would be the installation of a new President committed to the Fix and to the Radical Action Plan for implementing it. The Presidential Scenario could be combined with the Consuls Scenario, if the new President chose to appoint two consuls.

Two Consuls Scenario

One of the major dangers the country will face very soon is the tendency of people to grant sweeping new authority to a new strongman as a response to a tyrant they have just overthrown, and so they end up with another dictatorship.

An Historical Model: To counteract that threat, the successful rebels who overthrew the last Roman king (Tarquinius Superbus) in 509 BC and established the Roman Republic, set up a governing system that we might emulate as an interim solution. This system centered on the annual election of two consuls, who ruled in alternating months in collaboration with the Roman Senate; and each consul had veto power over the edicts of the other consul. This system lasted for over five centuries until Julius and then Augustus Caesar usurped the power of both the Senate and the consuls and established the Roman Empire in 27 AD. But 500 years ain't bad, and we only need a temporary system while we engineer a restored democracy.

So here is how our temporary Consular System of governance could work:

Two American Consuls resetting the republic

1. I suggest that we hire a Democrat and a Republican to govern jointly, both of whom are committed to democracy. Perhaps Liz Cheney and Eric Holder, or maybe John Kasich and Adam Schiff. Title each new temporary leader "Consul". The Consuls rule in alternating months, but each Consul has veto power over the acts of the other. Roman Consuls were elected annually. Ours should also rule for a maximum of one year.
2. In the U.S., the Consuls' main task is to implement the RAP, overseeing the system reset and leaving policy matters for the next elected government. The Consuls may take necessary emergency measures to keep the government running during this period. The Consuls should complete this task within one year and then cede power to the newly elected government under Constitution II.

Governors Scenario

A collection of Blue-state governors can force the issue by joint executive fiat. They need to declare that the Federal Government has abandoned the basic bargain which held the Union together for 2 ½ centuries, and that states are no longer receiving a fair shake. The governors can document an arm's length list of concrete examples. Accordingly, the Union has been suspended by the actions of the Feds. And beginning today, these states and businesses and citizens will no longer play the game – pay taxes, serve in the military, or follow Federal orders – until such time as the Feds get their act together. The governors will insist that the RAP be followed by the leaders in Washington, and, failing that, the governors themselves will begin implementing the RAP by convening a Constitution II Convention.

Citizens Scenario

As a last resort, if the other scenarios fail to materialize soon, then citizen activist leaders must emerge to implement the RAP themselves. Again, with loud and persistent public support, they can begin by calling for a Constitution II Convention...

RADICAL ACTION PLAN (RAP)

Whichever scenario is followed, the country's new leaders should implement the RAP to realize a new democracy in America.

Preparatory action before RAP can get underway: Get rid of Trump and guarantee that he will never return to office. I am somewhat stunned that I state this so boldly (I am not accustomed to taking such a radical position), but one full year of Trump's second term convinces me that we cannot be successful in achieving democratic reform as long as Trump remains President or the threat of Trump's return hangs over us. We know for certain that Donald Trump is a misogynist, racist, egotist, narcissist, rapist, vengeance seeking, mentally failing, convicted felon, liar, grifter, thief, and fraudster. He surrounds himself with others as bad as himself. As a businessman, he does not pay his bills or loans, and he has managed his way to six bankruptcies. His management style is incompetent and chaotic. His only achievement is having convinced voters twice to elect him President. So he must go, whether by resignation, impeachment and conviction, or natural death.

After Trump is put of the picture, our new leaders can implement the Rapid Action Plan, consisting of these steps:

1. Suspend the Supreme Court, pending the establishment of a new Federal Judiciary.

Old Congress Dissolved

2. Dissolve the House of Representatives, pending new elections from newly drawn Congressional Districts with non-gerrymandered boundaries. Dissolve the Senate, pending new elections from Senatorial Districts in each state with non-gerrymandered boundaries based on population.

Reverse Executive Orders

3. Reverse all Executive Orders issued by Trump 2. Also cancel Executive Orders issued by Trump 1 on a case basis.

Disqualify Insurrectionists

4. Disqualify anyone from serving in any public office who participated in, contributed to, or in any way gave material

support to the January 6, 2021, insurrection. This includes any member of Congress who voted to reject Electoral College votes on January 6 and any who voted to acquit Trump for his attempted coup. Any Federal or state level officials, whether elected or appointed, who supported Trump's attempted coup are likewise disqualified from further service to the United States or any state. (Important note: Other than disqualification to continue serving or to serve in the future, Trump and his supporters must not be prosecuted for their role in the January 6 insurrection or its subsequent denial or justification.)

Reinstate Federal Workers

5. Reinstate all Federal Executive Branch workers, programs, and agencies eliminated by Trump, except for those whose firings were approved by Congress and those disqualified from further service according to paragraph 4 above.

Electing Delegates to the Constitution II Convention

6. Immediately call on every state to elect delegates to the Constitution II Convention, with one delegate from each Congressional District. Candidates must live within the CD and may not currently hold any elected office or be an officer of any political party. Winners of this non-partisan election will be determined through Ranked Choice Voting.

Drafting Constitution II

7. The Constitution II Convention will draft Constitution II for the United States and will submit it to the country for ratification. Delegates will be informed by a constant stream of public opinion polls, so that the public is engaged and informed about and acquiesces with each article of the new document while deliberations are underway. When the Constitution II Convention completes its work, a plebiscite will be held throughout the United States to ratify the new Constitution II.

Ratification of Constitution II

8. Constitution II will be ratified if approved by a majority of voters in states whose populations make up 60% of the country. If ratified, it will go into effect in those states that have approved it. Because polling consistently shows that Americans of every political stripe prefer democracy over autocracy, and since the premise of Constitution II will be to more fully realize our democracy, I fully expect the citizens of every state to approve Constitution II. However, in the event that one or more states do not approve, then each state that has not approved it will have four choices: remain as a state under the new Constitution, remain in the United States as a US territory, join other states to form a new federation, or become an independent country. I really do not see that happening, but the breakup of the federation is a possible outcome.

9. Conduct the first elections under Constitution II for all Federal offices (President, Chancellor, and Congress). The temporary leaders (interim President, Consuls, Governors, or other) may not run for President in the initial Presidential election under Constitution II.

CONSULS CEDE POWER

10. The temporary leaders will cede authority to the first President elected under Constitution II.

CONSTITUTION II AND COMMENTARY

Constitution II must incorporate the protections, rights, and limits built into the existing document. It must prescribe fully democratic elections and representation in both chambers of Congress. It must mandate majority rule in all decisions in both chambers, with few exceptions. It must improve the checks and balances written into the 1787 Constitution. It must be amenable to amendment.

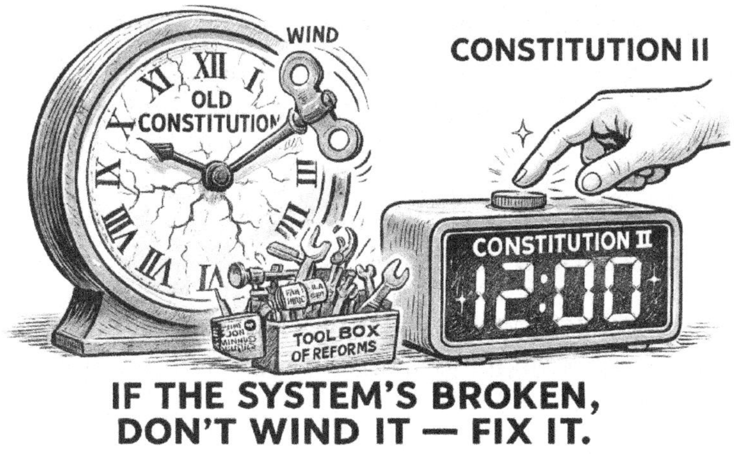

Out with the Old, In with the New

The document need not be lengthy or legalistic. Citizens should be able to read and understand it. And because Constitution II will be written in plain language, easily understood English, the Supreme Court must only interpret it according to the plain language meaning written into it. They will not need to force interpretations of ideas that might be implied, because the means of amending Constitution II will also be far less daunting than is the case at present.

I have consciously written this as a Midlander, part of the mostly-Blue states coalition. I do believe that a clear majority of Americans subscribe to the underlying principles presented here, but you will be the judge of that. Constitution II favors neither political party, but it does favor democracy over authoritarianism. For example, after 1876, Jim Crow laws and other voter suppression techniques dramatically reduced voter participation throughout the former Confederacy. I view this negatively. To solve this problem, Constitution II requires all adults to vote in every election.

You can be a conservative or a liberal, or of any other ideological persuasion; you can be Republican or Democrat, or of any other political party or no party at all; but in all of these cases, we should all be able to agree that your voice is important, your vote is important, and you deserve to be heard.

The rest of this document is one man's rough draft of Constitution II for the United States of America, along with commentary where needed to describe the differences between the proposed draft and the existing Constitution.

Provisions copied from the 1787 Constitution appear in normal type; ***new wording is in bold italics.***

In several instances, modern words and phrases replace outdated ones without changing the meaning. These appear in normal type.

> COMMENTARY Starts with the COMMENTARY, appears in this odd font (Agency FB), indented,, with a double-line before and after each comment.

CONSTITUTION II

PREAMBLE

We the People of the United States, in order to form a more perfect union, establish Justice, ensure domestic tranquility, provide for the common defense, promote the general welfare, and secure the blessings of liberty to ourselves and our posterity, do ordain and establish Constitution ***II*** for the United States of America.

Preamble

STIPULATIONS

Constitution II replaces the United States Constitution of 1787, as amended.

Constitution II establishes a Federal Government consisting of three co-equal branches: the Legislative, the Executive, and the Judicial.

COMMENTARY: Although we often refer to three co-equal branches of government, the notion is nowhere stated in the 1787 Constitution. Let's make it explicit.

Article 0: Bill of Rights

COMMENTARY: Some of the most significant and oft-referenced provisions of the 1787 Constitution appear in the first ten Amendments, usually called the Bill of Rights. These rights are so fundamental that it seems reasonable to state them first, at the very beginning of Constitution II. They are no longer amendments or add-ons to the document, but rather they are integral to the whole thing. Grouping these rights under Article 0 accomplishes two objectives: It emphasizes that these rights are pre-eminent and pertain to the entire Constitution II, and it allows us to preserve the implied hierarchical order of the three co-equal branches of government as Article I – Legislative, Article II- Executive, and Article III – Judicial.

Section 1: Introduction to the Bill of Rights

1.1 Basis of All Rights

The United States of America is a representative democracy with a limited free market economy. The principles of democracy (majority rule, limited government, belief in democracy, a free press, and truth in official government speech) underlie the government structures laid out in Constitution II and form the basis for the limits on the Government's ability to regulate personal private behavior. Congress has broad power to regulate commerce.

America's populace is a diverse mix of all races, ethnicities, religions, ages, genders, orientations, wealth, income, and education levels. This diversity is our strength. We are also a nation of immigrants, another significant strength. In addition to recognizing and accepting diversity, we also strive for equity (equality of opportunity, not equality of outcomes) and inclusion (representatives of all groups get a seat at the table). Hence, DEI programs are foundational to the proper functioning of our democracy .

1.2 Categories of Rights

This Bill of Rights establishes the rights of natural persons, of citizens, and of states. The Federal Government and the several states may also recognize rights of other legal entities,

such as corporations, partnerships, trusts, charities, and benevolent associations; but such rights are not constitutionally guaranteed.

COMMENTARY: In the *Citizens United* decision, the Supreme Court stated that corporations are people too. Article 0 Section 1.2 specifically overturns the justification for that erroneous decision, that is, corporations are not people.

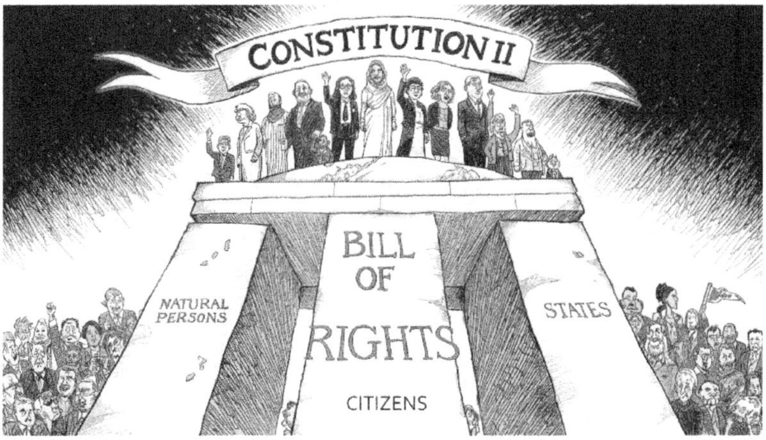

Bill of Rights

1.3 Right to Delegate Powers

The Federal Government may delegate any of its powers to the several states. A collection of states may delegate any of their powers to the Federal Government. A collection of states may also create a public agency to jointly execute certain state powers, and may request the Federal Government to participate or support such public agencies. In none of these cases do any of the parties involved irrevocably concede any of their powers to another component of government.

COMMENTARY: This provision insures that the Federal government and state governments may effectively cooperate with each other without running afoul of the Separation of Powers doctrine.

1.4 Retention of Rights

The enumeration in Constitution II of certain rights shall not be construed to deny or disparage others retained by the people.

The powers not delegated to the United States by Constitution II, nor prohibited by it to the states, are reserved to the states respectively, or to the people.

Section 2: Bill of Rights of Natural Persons

2.1 Equality of All Natural Persons

All natural persons are created equal, and are born with certain inalienable rights, and among these rights are life, liberty, property, and the pursuit of happiness. These rights are guaranteed to all natural persons from birth to death.

> COMMENTARY: Again, corporations are not people. Constitution II guarantees people's rights from birth to death.

2.2 Freedom of Religion, Press, and Expression

Congress shall make no law respecting an establishment of religion, or prohibiting the free exercise thereof; or abridging the freedom of speech, or of the press; or the right of the people peaceably to assemble, and to petition the Government for a redress of grievances.

2.3 Freedom from Discrimination

Discrimination against any person on the basis of sex, race, ethnicity, religion, or sexual orientation or identity is prohibited.

Discrimination against any person on the basis of age, between ages 40 and 70, is prohibited.

2.4 Prohibition of Slavery

Neither slavery nor involuntary servitude, except as a punishment for crime whereof the party shall have been duly convicted, shall exist within the United States, or any place subject to its jurisdiction.

2.5 Prohibition on Cruel and Unusual Punishments, ***on Torture, and on Capital Punishment***

Excessive bail shall not be required, nor excessive fines imposed, nor cruel and unusual punishments inflicted.

No Torture

The United States does not practice or tolerate the use of torture. The intentional infliction of extreme pain upon any person for the purpose of obtaining information, for punishment, or for any other purpose, is prohibited.

Except as punishment for treason, the Unites States does not inflict capital punishment.

No Capital Punishment

2.6 Search and Seizure

The right of the people to be secure in their persons, houses, papers, and effects, against unreasonable searches and seizures, shall not be violated, and no warrant shall issue, but upon probable cause, supported by oath or affirmation, and particularly describing the place to be searched, and the persons or things to be seized. ***A warrant can only be issued by a judge.***

Right to Privacy

Any government agent (Federal, state, or local) executing a search warrant, effecting an arrest, or detaining any person for any reason must show their face and identify themselves, their photo ID, identification number, and the agency they represent.

COMMENTARY: The first sentence of the Search and Seizure clause is copied from the 4th Amendment to the 1787 Constitution. The 2nd and 3rd sentences could be inferred from the 1st sentence, but the abuses of the Trump presidency, especially those committed by ICE, make the 2nd and 3rd sentences necessary.)

2.7 Privacy

All persons have a right to privacy, and the right to be free from libel, slander, and other false defamation.

COMMENTARY: When the Government –specifically the President or the Justice Department – libels or slanders an individual person or group, the aggrieved party should be able to seek redress, but redress only becomes possible because Constitution II specifically states that such aggressive tactics by the Government are unconstitutional.

Section 3: Bill of Rights of Citizens

3.1 Definition of Citizens

Two categories of citizens are recognized: a natural-born citizen and a naturalized citizen:

Citizenship

- ***A natural-born citizen is any person***
  - ***Who was born within the United States, its territories, possessions, or* U.S. Government jurisdiction, or**
  - ***Whose biological mother or father was an American citizen at the time of the child's birth. To retain natural-born citizenship under this provision after one's 21st birthday, a natural-born citizen not born in the United States must notify the Secretary of State***

of the United States, between their 18th and 21st birthdays, of their intent to remain an American citizen.

- ***A naturalized citizen is any person who becomes an American citizen in accordance with the Federal law regulating the naturalization process.***
- ***With the sole exception of eligibility to hold the office of President of the United States, which requires the President to be a natural-born citizen, no distinction shall be made between natural-born and naturalized citizens.***
- ***An American citizen may obtain or maintain citizenship in another country while remaining an American citizen.***
- ***The Government does not have the power to take citizenship away from any citizen.***

COMMENTARY: Despite the guarantee of birthright citizenship in the 14th Amendment to the 1787 Constitution, some recent debate has arisen around this concept. The purpose of Article 0 Section 3.1 is to re-establish birthright citizenship as a bedrock principle of being an American.

3.2 Right to Bear Arms

Right to Bear Arms

For reasons of personal safety, hunting, and/or recreation, a citizen has the right to keep and bear personal weapons, including firearms appropriate to such purposes.

COMMENTARY: Article 0 Section3.2 enshrines the Second amendment to the 1787 Constitution within Constitution II. It properly separates the citizen's right to bear arms from the right of states to maintain a militia, which is a different subject. It also specifies the legal reasons for owning a firearm, as well as the types of firearms that can be permitted.

3.3 Quartering of Soldiers

No Soldier shall be quartered in any house in time of peace, without the consent of the owner, nor in time of war, but in a manner to be prescribed by law.

3.4 Trial and Punishment; Compensation for Takings

No person shall be held to answer for a capital, or otherwise infamous crime, unless on a presentment or indictment of a grand jury, except in cases arising in the land or naval forces, or in the militia, when in actual service in time of war or public danger; nor shall any person be subject for the same offense to be twice put in jeopardy of life or limb; nor shall be compelled in any criminal case to be a witness against himself, nor be deprived of life, liberty, or property, without due process of law; nor shall private property be taken for public use, without just compensation. ***No citizen shall be forced to surrender private property for private gain; the principle and legal process of eminent domain shall only be used to serve a demonstrated public need.***

COMMENTARY: Article 0 Section3.4 repeats the basic rules concerning eminent domain. The last sentence reinforces the notion that eminent domain can only be used to serve a public need (not private gain). This clarification seems to be needed because of recent debates concerning the use of eminent domain to acquire private land for privately-owned pipelines, transmission lines, and toll roads.

Limits on Eminent Domain

3.5 Right to Speedy Trial; Confrontation of Witnesses; Assistance of Counsel

In all criminal prosecutions, the accused shall enjoy the right to a speedy and public trial, by an impartial jury of the state and district wherein the crime shall have been committed, which district shall have been previously ascertained by law, and to be informed of the nature and cause of the accusation; to be confronted with the witnesses against him; to have compulsory process for obtaining witnesses in his favor, and to have the assistance of counsel for his defense.

3.6 Trial by Jury in Civil Cases

In suits at common law, where the value in controversy shall exceed ***$1000***, the right of trial by jury shall be preserved, and no fact tried by a jury, shall be otherwise reexamined in any court of the United States, than according to the rules of the common law.

3.7 Social Safety Net.

Health Education, and Basic Necessities

Citizens of all ages have a right to tax-supported medical care, education, basic necessities of life, and safety, including:

- ***medically necessary healthcare, including physicians, hospitals, medicines, medical devices, all reproductive services (abortion, pre-natal care, obstetrics), dental, vision, hearing, hospice, and mental health services;***
- ***public education (according to the education standards established by Congress) from pre-school through graduate school and lifelong learning, as well as public libraries;***

- ***the necessities of life – food, clothing, and shelter – sufficient to prevent death from starvation and exposure to the elements; and***
- ***public safety: police, fire, and rescue).***

The citizen rights in this section shall be provided by the state in which each citizen resides, in partnership with the Federal Government.

COMMENTARY: Other than the new election procedures in Article V, Section 3.7 of Article O may be the most significant change in Constitution II from the 1787 Constitution. This section states that medical care, education, the social safety net, and public safety will all be provided as public services – as they are in every other modern democracy. The public, I believe, will overwhelmingly support this program.

3.8 Equal Protection of the Laws

Diversity, Equity, and Inclusion are foundational values of the United States and foundational to the equal protection of the laws. No state shall make or enforce any law which shall abridge the privileges or immunities of citizens of the United States; nor shall any state deprive any person of life, liberty, or property, without due process of law; nor deny to any person within its jurisdiction the equal protection of the laws.

COMMENTARY: DEI must be mandated in our Constitution and belongs most appropriately in the Bill of Rights.

Section 4: Bill of Rights of States

4.1 Voluntary Union of states

- ***The United States of America is a voluntary union of those states whose citizens have ratified Constitution II and have therefore agreed to join the Union and be subject to its jurisdiction.***

COMMENTARY: Citizens of each state have the right to join the Union, which they will do by ratifying Constitution II.

- ***In addition to the 50 states in the Union under the 1787 Constitution, citizens of the District of Columbia and the Territory of Puerto Rico also each have the right to voluntarily join the Union by ratifying Constitution II.***

COMMENTARY: Racism, religious bigotry, and politics have prevented Washington, DC and Puerto Rico from becoming states for at least 50 years, maybe 100 years. The District of Columbia's population is largely black, which disqualifies it from statehood in the minds of racists. Puerto Rico's citizens violate three norms of the America Firsters: they are non-white, they are Catholic, and they speak Spanish. Politically, Republicans fear that four new Senators would all be Democrats – but that's with the unfair Senatorial representation model in the 1787 Constitution. Perhaps Republicans would have a better shot at capturing one or two new Senators from DC an Puerto Rico if the Senate representation were fair, as it will be under Constitution II.

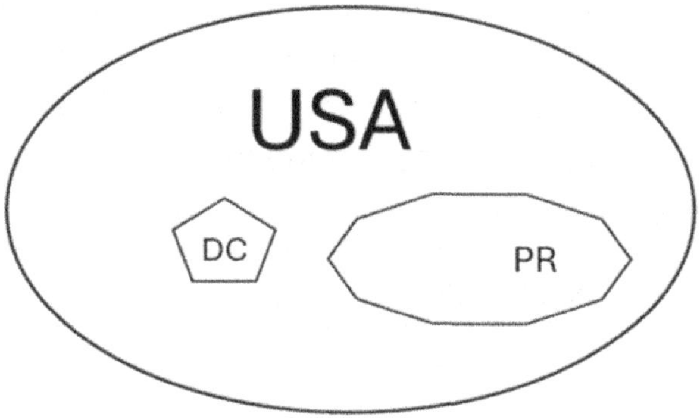

Welcome to the Union: Washington, DC, and Puerto Rico

- New states may be admitted by the Congress into this Union; but no new states shall be formed or erected within the jurisdiction of any other state; nor any state be formed by the junction of two or more states, or parts of states, without the consent of the ***voters and*** legislatures of the states concerned as well as of the Congress.

COMMENTARY: In addition to state legislators, voter should also have a say.

4.2 Secession

Any state may, by a majority vote of its citizens and its legislature, give notice of its intention to secede from the Union. If approved by the people in a second plebiscite, held not less than five nor more than seven years after the initial notice to separate is given, then that state shall no longer be a part of the Union.

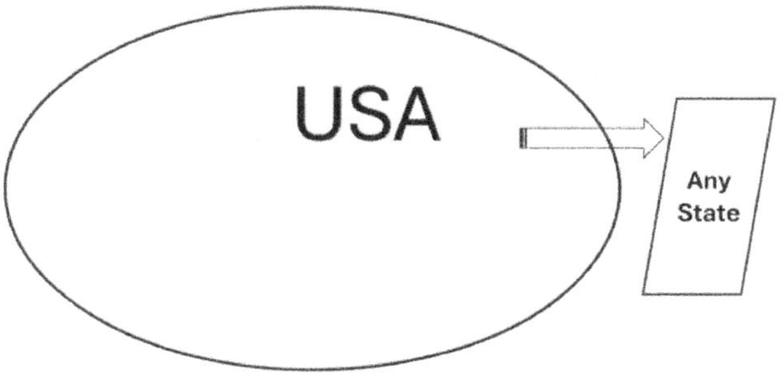

Goodbye to Any State That Wants to Leave

COMMENTARY: Perhaps if a secession procedure had been included in the 1787 Constitution, the Civil War could have been avoided.

4.3 Each State to Honor All Others

Full faith and credit shall be given in each state to the public acts, records, and judicial proceedings of every other state. And the Congress may by general laws prescribe the manner in which such acts, records and proceedings shall be proved, and the effect thereof.

4.4 State Citizens, Extradition

The citizens of each state shall be entitled to all privileges and immunities of citizens in the several states.

A person charged in any state with treason, felony, or other crime, who shall flee from justice, and be found in another state, shall on demand of the executive authority of the state from which they fled, be delivered up, to be removed to the state having jurisdiction of the crime.

4.5 Representative Democracy

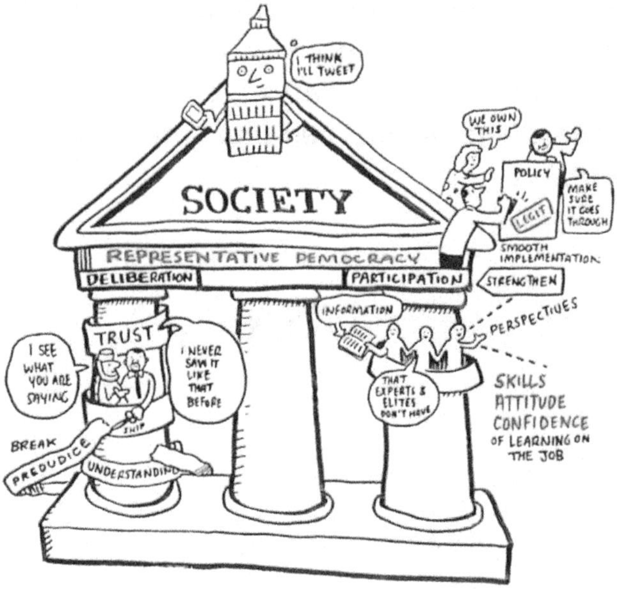

Representative Democracy in Every State

The United States shall guarantee to every state in this Union a ***representative democracy*** form of government, and shall protect each of them against invasion; and, on application of the executive authority of the state, against domestic violence.

COMMENTARY: "Representative democracy" seems a much better phrasing than "republican".

4.6 State Militia

State Militia

A well-regulated militia being necessary to the security of a free state, the right of ***each state*** to keep and bear arms shall not be infringed.

COMMENTARY: This section restores the Second Amendment to its original civic context. The Framers' intent was to ensure that each state could maintain a trained and armed militia as a safeguard against tyranny and invasion—not to guarantee unrestricted private gun ownership. Over time, that intent has been distorted into an individual entitlement detached from the idea of a "well-regulated militia." Constitution II restores the clause to its original meaning by affirming the collective right of each state to organize, arm, and regulate its militia for the defense of a free state. The right of individual citizens to own personal firearms for safety, hunting, and recreation is separately guaranteed in Article 0 Section 3.2, where it properly belongs among the rights of citizens rather than those of states.

4.7 Social Safety Net

Every state has the authority and responsibility to provide to its residents the social services specified in Article 0 Section 3.7. The several states may request assistance from the Federal Government to exercise this power.

COMMENTARY: States will not be able to argue that they do not have the authority to provide publicly supported medical care, public education, social safety net, or public safety, because Constitution II Article D Section 4.7 gives states the power to do precisely these things.

Article I: The Legislative Branch

Section 1: The Legislature

All legislative powers herein granted shall be vested in a Congress of the United States, which shall consist of a ***lower chamber, known as the House of Representatives, and an upper chamber, known as the Senate.***

Both chambers shall consist of members chosen from the several states and from the Non-State Election District in accordance with Article V -- Elections.

COMMENTARY: Under Constitution II, American citizens who do not reside in any state are nevertheless permitted to vote for all Federal offices. They vote for President, Chancellor (former vice President), and for one member of the House and one member of the Senate. This provision gives several million American expats a voice in Congress.

In each chamber, each member shall have one vote. And every decision made in each chamber shall be made by majority vote, except where Constitution II specifies otherwise.

COMMENTARY: This provision eliminates the filibuster as well as indefinite "holds" on Senate confirmation votes and similar tactics.. (Remember that the first pillar of democracy is "Majority Rule".) [Note: the effective substitute for the filibuster appears in Article I Section 7.]

Section 2: The House of Representatives

2.1 Eligibility

When a Representative takes office, they must be

- At least 25 years old
- At least 7 years a citizen of the United States
- ***Less than 19 years a Member of the House of Representatives and***
- A resident of the state from which they were chosen.

COMMENTARY: Constitution II includes term limits for all Federal officials: President, Chancellor, Senator, Representative, and Judge. The term limit for House Members limits them to 10 terms (20 years).

2.2 Vacancies

When vacancies happen in the representation from any state, the executive authority thereof shall issue writs of election to fill such vacancies.

2.3 Officers; Power of Impeachment

The House of Representatives shall choose their Speaker and other officers; and the House shall have the sole power of impeachment.

Section 3 – The Senate

3.1 Presiding Officer

The Chancellor of the Senate shall preside over the Senate. The Chancellor shall be elected for a four-year term of office in accordance with Article V – Elections. The Chancellor shall have one vote on all matters that come before the Senate, the same as any Senator.

When the Chancellor of the Senate takes office, they must meet the same eligibility criteria as the President of the United States.

COMMENTARY: The position of Chancellor of the Senate replaces the position of Vice President of the United States. The Chancellor has more responsibility that the Vice President ever had, is elected directly by the people, and serves without any official tie to the President. The Chancellor position is a major part of the restructuring in Constitution II designed to move away from the "Imperial Presidency", but without diminishing the authority of the President to direct the Executive Branch.

3.2 Eligibility

When a Senator takes office, they must be

- At least 30 years old
- At least 9 years a citizen of the United States
- ***Less than 18 years a Senator and***
- A resident of the state from which they were chosen.

COMMENTARY: The term limit for Senate Members limits them to 4 terms (20 years), as you will see in Article V Section 3.1.

3.3 Vacancies

When vacancies happen in the representation from any state, the executive authority thereof shall issue writs of election to fill such vacancies.

3.4 Officers; Power of Impeachment

The ***Chancellor*** shall appoint a Senate ***Chancellor*** Pro Tempore, with the concurrence of a majority of Senators present and voting. The Senate ***Chancellor*** Pro Tempore shall preside over the Senate in the absence of the ***Chancellor***, or when the ***Chancellor*** shall exercise the Office of President of the United States.

The Senate shall have the sole power to try all impeachments. When the President ***or Chancellor*** is tried, the Chief Justice shall preside, *and* ***judicial rules and procedure will be followed***: And no person shall be convicted without the concurrence of two-thirds of the members present.

COMMENTARY: This clause makes it clear that the Chief Justice does not just convene the impeachment trial but actually presides over it.

Judgement in cases of impeachment ***includes*** removal from office and disqualification to hold and enjoy any office of honor, trust or profit under the United States: but the party convicted shall nevertheless be liable and subject to indictment, trial, judgment and punishment, according to law.

COMMENTARY: This rewording means that conviction of an impeached official involves both removal from office AND disqualification from further service to the United States Government.

Section 4 - Meetings

The Congress shall assemble at least once every year, and such meeting shall commence on ***December 1***, unless Congress shall by law appoint a different day.

COMMENTARY: From the election to the new Congress is only two weeks, leaving no time for a lame duck session of Congress – a salutary effect of convening the new Congress on December 1.

When Congress is in session, it shall meet on designated legislative days, specifically on Wednesdays through Sundays

from 4pm to 10pm, except Federal holidays, unless Congress adopts a different schedule.

COMMENTARY: This schedule requires Congress to meet when most working Americans are able to watch, The British House of Commons sits in session afternoons and evenings Monday through Friday, so the schedule in Constitution II is similar, though meeting on weekends and having Mondays and Tuesdays off is an innovation.

Either chamber, when it does not meet with a quorum of members present for three consecutive legislative days, shall be deemed to be in recess.

COMMENTARY: This provision prevents Congress from pretending to meet with only a few members present, in order to avoid going into recess.

In even-numbered years (that is, election years), Congress shall adjourn sine die no later than July 4, and shall not reconvene until a new Congress convenes following the election.

COMMENTARY: To adjourn "sine die" means that no date is set to return and marks the end of this Congressional session. This provision allows members to focus on campaigning during the months leading up to an election. And since Congress will not meet from July 4 through December 1, the "lame duck" session is eliminated.

Section 5 - Membership, Rules, Journals, and Adjournment

Each chamber shall be the Judge of the elections, returns and qualifications of its own members, and a majority of each shall constitute a quorum to do business; but a smaller number may adjourn from day to day, and may be authorized to compel the attendance of absent members, in such manner, and under such penalties as each chamber may provide.

Any member may make a motion to call a bill, a resolution, or an appointment to the floor for a vote; and, if a majority of members present concur, that bill, resolution, or appointment shall become the first order of business in that chamber on the next legislative day; and at that time, such bill, resolution, or appointment will, by majority vote, be either approved, disapproved, or tabled for later consideration.

COMMENTARY: This is another provision designed to ensure majority rule.

Each chamber may determine the rules of its proceedings, punish its members for disorderly behavior, and, with the concurrence of two-thirds, expel a member.

Each chamber shall keep a Journal of its proceedings, and from time to time publish the same, excepting such parts as may in their judgment require secrecy; and the yeas and nays of the members of either chamber on any question shall, at the desire of one fifth of those present, be entered on the journal.

Neither chamber, during the session of Congress, shall, without the consent of the other, adjourn for more than three days, nor to any other place than that in which the two chambers shall be sitting.

Section 6 - Compensation

Senators and Representatives shall receive a compensation for their services, to be ascertained by law, and paid out of the Treasury of the United States. However, no law varying the compensation for the services of the Senators and Representatives shall take effect, until an election of Representatives shall have intervened.

No Senator or Representative shall, during the time for which he was elected, be appointed to any office under the authority of the United States or any state which shall have been created, or the emoluments whereof shall have been increased during such time; and no person holding any office under the United States shall be a member of either chamber during their continuance in office.

Senators and Representatives shall in all cases, except treason, felony and breach of the peace, be privileged from arrest during their attendance at the session of their respective chambers, and in going to and returning from the same; and for any speech or debate in either chamber, they shall not be questioned in any other place.

Section 7 - Revenue Bills, Legislative Process, and Presidential Veto

All bills for raising revenue shall originate in the House of Representatives; but the Senate may propose or concur with amendments as on other bills.

The earliest effective date of any bill, when enacted by Congress, shall be July 1st following the next Congressional election after passage of the bill. An earlier effective date can only be enacted if (1) the sole purpose of the bill is to repeal a bill which has not yet gone into effect, or (2) an earlier date is agreed to by three-fifths of members present in both chambers upon final passage of the bill.

COMMENTARY: This provision eliminates the need for a filibuster to delay action on a bill until "the people exercise their right to weigh in". It also extends to both chambers the same privilege to pass emergency legislation with a super majority, but to enact normal legislation by a simple majority vote.

Every Bill which shall have passed the House of Representatives and the Senate, shall, before it becomes a law, be presented to the President of the United States; If they approve the bill, they shall sign it, but if not they shall return it, with their objections to that chamber in which it shall have originated, who shall enter the objections at large on their journal, and proceed to reconsider it. If after such reconsideration two-thirds of that chamber shall agree to pass the bill, it shall be sent, together with the objections, to the other chamber, by which it shall likewise be reconsidered, and if approved by two-thirds of that chamber, it shall become a law. But in all such cases the votes of both chambers shall be determined by yeas and nays, and the names of the persons voting for and against the bill shall be entered on the journal of each chamber respectively. If any bill shall not be returned by the President within ten *legislative* days after it shall have been presented to them, the same shall be a law, in like manner as if they had signed it, unless the Congress by their adjournment prevent its return, in which case it shall not be a law.

Every order, resolution, or vote to which the concurrence of the Senate and House of Representatives may be necessary (except on a question of adjournment) shall be presented to the President of the United States; and before the same shall take effect, shall be approved by him, or being disapproved by him, shall be repassed by two-thirds of the Senate and House of Representatives, according to the rules and limitations prescribed in the case of a bill.

Section 8 - Powers of Congress

Congress shall have power as follows:

COMMENTARY: This enumeration of Congressional powers is slightly more expansive than the list in the 1787 Constitution. One must note, however, that giving Congress the authority to do something does not imply that Congress SHOULD do something. What it does mean is that members of Congress can pass legislation in this area without running into objections that such a measure is unconstitutional because Congress lacks the power to legislate on that subject.

To lay and collect taxes, duties or tariffs, imposts and excises, to pay the debts and provide for the common defense and general welfare of the United States; but all duties, imposts and excises shall be uniform throughout the United States;

To lay and collect taxes on incomes, from whatever source derived, without apportionment among the several states, and without regard to any census or enumeration.

To borrow money on the credit of the United States;

To regulate commerce with foreign nations, and among the several states, and with the Indian Tribes;

To establish a uniform rule of naturalization, and uniform laws on the subject of bankruptcies throughout the United States;

To coin money, regulate the value thereof, and of foreign coin, and fix the standard of weights and measures;

To provide for the punishment of counterfeiting the securities and current coin of the United States;

To establish post offices;

To conduct a census of the United States a***t the beginning of every decade, that is, during years ending in 0;***

COMMENTARY: This clause clarifies when the decennial census must take place.

To promote the progress of science and useful arts, ***by conducting and sponsoring scientific research and cultural and artistic endeavors;***

COMMENTARY: This clause makes explicit Congress's power to promote science and culture.

To secure for limited times to authors and inventors the exclusive right to their respective writings and discoveries, ***provided,***

however, that copyright protection shall not exceed 50 years, and patent protection shall not exceed 25 years;

COMMENTARY: This new limitation on Congressional power is a response to Congress' abuse of that power in recent decades.

To constitute tribunals inferior to the Supreme Court;

To define and punish *crimes* committed on the high seas, ***in outer space, in cyberspace, or in any place not subject to the jurisdiction of any nation***, and offenses against international law;

COMMENTARY: This language replaces the outdated terminology in the 1787 Constitution but does not change its meaning.

To declare war, authorize military proxies, and make rules concerning captures wherever they may occur;

COMMENTARY: Updated wording

To raise and support the Armed Forces of the United States (on land, on sea, in the air, ***and in cyber space***);

To make rules for the government and regulation of the Armed Forces;

To provide for calling forth state militia to execute the laws of the Union, suppress Insurrections, and repel Invasions;

To provide for organizing, arming, and disciplining the state militia, and for governing such part of them as may be employed in the service of the United States, reserving to the states respectively, the appointment of the officers, and the authority of training the militia according to the discipline prescribed by Congress;

Feds set standards; states run the schools

To establish standards and guidelines for public education, including a national curriculum, standards for accreditation of schools and teachers, and guidelines for student achievement and advancement, while reserving to the states respectively the operation of the education system in accordance with the standards established by Congress. The national curriculum must emphasize factual history, civics, the value of representative democracy, math and science, and useful arts and trades;

COMMENTARY: The right to free public education at all ages is guaranteed by the Bill of Rights, Article 0. Section 3.7. This clause gives Congress the power to legislate concerning national educational standards

EPA Mission

To protect the environment, and to provide for public health and safety by ensuring access to clean and safe water, air, energy, medicines, and the food supply;

COMMENTARY: This new clause makes it clear that Congress is empowered to protect the environment. Again, it does not mandate that Congress legislate in this arena; it just gives Congress the clear authority to do so if Congress so chooses.

To provide financial assistance to the several states, based on the unique needs of each state, for infrastructure projects, for emergency relief from natural disasters, for fulfillment of each state's obligations under Article 0 Section 3.7, and for such other purposes as Congress may deem appropriate and necessary;

COMMENTARY: This clause clarifies Congress' power to assist states when needed (FEMA, Coast Guard, Social Safety Net).

Enabling Medicare for All

To provide publicly-funded medical care for all citizens, in partnership with the states[

COMMENTARY: Expanding on Medicare, Medicaid, and the Veterans Administration, Congress will now have the power to design and implement a public medical care system for the United States, bringing us in line with all other developed nations in the world.

Enabling Campaign finance Reform

To provide public financing for Federal elections and election campaigns, to regulate and limit campaign contributions, and to mandate full disclosure of the sources and amounts of campaign contributions;

COMMENTARY: This new clause gives Congress the power to regulate campaign financing.

To regulate all Federal elections in accordance with Article V, provided that the actual conduct of the elections is left to the states; and to modify by law any of the provisions of Article V, provided two-thirds of members present in each chamber agree;

COMMENTARY: This new clause grants to Congress the power to regulate Federal elections, which are conducted by the states. To alter Constitutional provisions regarding elections requires a super-majority, since such action would override provisions which the citizens have already approved.

To dispose of and make all needful rules and regulations respecting the territory or other property belonging to the United States, including all places purchased by the consent of the legislature of the state in which the same shall be, for the erection of forts, magazines, arsenals, dockyards, and other needful buildings;

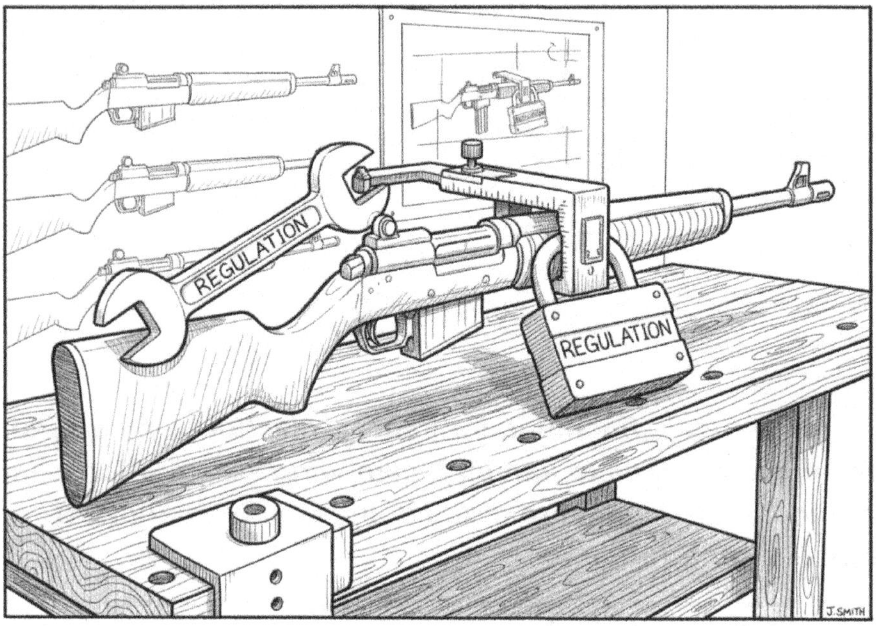

To regulate firearms in accordance with Article 0 Section 3.2.

COMMENTARY: Giving Congress this power explicitly is an important corollary to giving citizens the right to bear arms.

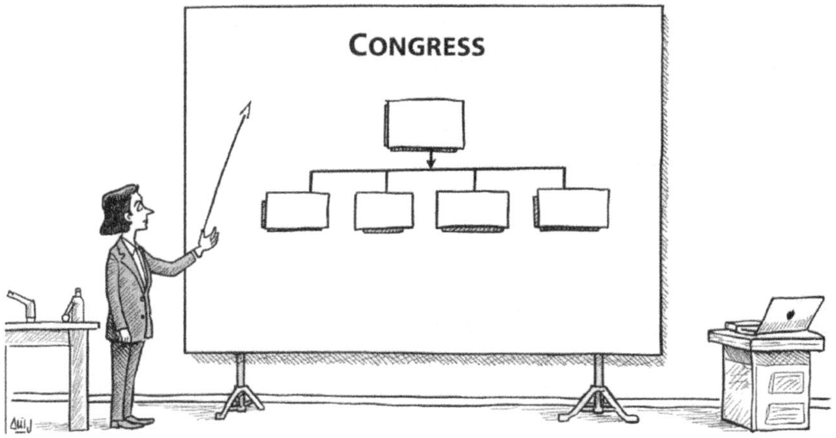

To make all laws regarding the organization of Cabinet-level Executive Departments, other Executive Branch entities, and independent agencies, including the establishment or abolishment of each department and program and assigning its mission, functions, structure, and budget;

COMMENTARY: This clause clarifies the power of Congress to mandate the structure of Executive Branch entities. The President has no corresponding powers.

To make all laws pertaining to Executive Branch entities disestablished after 2024. Until Congress acts under Constitution II, such entities continue in existence, and the laws and regulations pertaining to these entities remain in full force and effect;

COMMENTARY: Trump and his illegal puppet "agency" DOGE illegally attempted to do away with the United States Agency for International Development, the Voice of America, the Department of Education, the Consumer finance Protection Bureau, and many other Federal Government components. These entities remain in existence until the new Congress decides otherwise.

And

To make all laws which shall be necessary and proper for carrying into execution the foregoing powers, and all other powers vested by Constitution II in the Government of the United States, or in any department or officer thereof.

Section 9 - Limits on Congress

The privilege of the writ of habeas corpus shall not be suspended, ***unless by Act of Congress*** when the public safety may require it due to rebellion or invasion.

COMMENTARY: A writ of *habeas corpus* is a demand issued by a court to an executive over whom the court has jurisdiction, demanding that the executive bring to the court someone whom the executive is holding in confinement, and requiring the executive to explain to the court the legal justification for continuing to confine that person. This provision, including the suspension of the privilege during a rebellion or invasion, is based on British precedent.

This clause also states that the privilege of *habeas corpus* cannot be suspended "unless by Act of Congress". This phrase insures that only Congress has the power to suspend the privilege of the writ of habeas corpus. (In the past, this power has been exercised by the President.) The idea, again, is to rein in the Imperial Presidency.

No bill of attainder or ex post facto law shall be passed.

COMMENTARY: A *bill of attainder* makes a person or group guilty of treason or other capital offense without a trial, and also takes away the civil rights, property, and titles of the person "attainted".

An *ex post facto* law is a law that criminalizes behavior that occurred before the law was passed.

No tax or duty shall be laid on articles exported from any state.

No preference shall be given by any regulation of commerce or revenue to the ports of one state over those of another: nor shall vessels bound to, or from, one state, be obliged to enter, clear, or pay duties in another.

Congress shall not prohibit alcohol or mood-altering substances in any state where state law permits them.

COMMENTARY: States can permit or restrict such substances.

BALANCED BUDGET MANDATE

No money shall be drawn from the Treasury, but in consequence of appropriations made by law; and a regular statement and account of the receipts and expenditures of all public money shall be published from time to time.

Expenditures from the U.S. Treasury authorized by Congress for any fiscal year shall not exceed revenues received into the U.S. Treasury during the previous fiscal year. Congress may make exceptions to this expenditure restriction, limited to one fiscal year at a time.

COMMENTARY: This new provision mandates a balanced budget, for many years a cherished objective of fiscal conservatives. Leftists always claim that oligarchs are bankrupting the country through tax-breaks, corporate subsidies, and sweetheart contracts. Righties always claim that the lefties are bankrupting the country through social programs the country cannot afford. This balanced budget clause does not prevent either side from giving away the store, but it does insure that we pay for it as we go, whatever fiscal policies are adopted.

The Federal Government does not register voters, maintain voter rolls, or conduct Federal elections (these are all functions of the several states) – except that the US Secretary of State shall conduct elections for the Non-State Election District (see Article V, Section 1.2).

No title of nobility shall be granted by the United States: And no person holding any office of profit or trust under the United States shall, without the consent of Congress, accept of any present, emolument, office, title, or ***payment***, of any kind whatever, from any king, prince, foreign state, ***or other foreign person or entity.***

COMMENTARY: This phrasing extends the "no foreign emoluments" clause to include gifts from corporations or individuals.

Section 10 - Powers prohibited of states

No state shall enter into any treaty, alliance, or confederation; authorize privateers or other military proxies for the state; coin money; emit bills of credit; pass any bill of attainder, ex post facto law, or law impairing the obligation of contracts, or grant any title of nobility.

No state shall, without the consent of Congress, lay any imposts or duties on imports or exports, except what may be absolutely necessary for executing its inspection laws: and the net produce of all duties and imposts, laid by any state on imports or exports, shall be for the use of the Treasury of the United States; and all such laws shall be subject to the revision and control of Congress.

No state shall, without the consent of Congress, lay any duty of tonnage, keep troops, or ships of war in time of peace, enter into any agreement or compact with another state, or with a foreign power, or engage in war, unless actually invaded, or in such imminent danger as will not admit of delay.

Article II: The Executive Branch

Section 1 - The President

1.1 The executive power shall be vested in a President of the United States of America, who will serve a four-year term of office and will be elected ***in accordance with Article V – Elections. No person shall be elected President more than twice, and no person shall serve as President for more than 10 years, including time served as Acting President or as a successor to another President.***

COMMENTARY: This clause fixes a small oversight in the existing Constitution, which in certain circumstances could allow a president to serve a third term.

1.2 Eligibility for the Office of President: Upon taking office, the President must be

- At least 35 years old*;*
- A natural-born citizen of the United States;
- At least 14 years a resident within the United States; and
- Less than 6 years the President of the United States.

1.3 Lack of a qualified President elect: If, at the time fixed for the beginning of the term of the President, the President elect shall have died, the ***Chancellor*** shall become President. If a President elect shall not have qualified, then the ***Chancellor*** shall act as President until a President shall have qualified.

1.4 Vacancy in the office of President:

a) In case of the removal of the President from office or of his death or resignation, the ***Chancellor*** shall become President. After the ***Chancellor***, the line of succession to the Presidency is the Speaker of the House, the ***Chancellor*** Pro Tempore of the Senate, the Secretary of State, and the remaining cabinet members in the order in which their departments were created by Congress.
b) Whenever the President transmits to the ***Chancellor*** Pro Tempore of the Senate and the Speaker of the House of Representatives his written declaration that he is unable to discharge the powers and duties of his office, and until he transmits to them a written declaration to the contrary, such powers and duties shall be discharged by the ***Chancellor*** as Acting President.
c) Whenever the ***Chancellor*** and a majority of either the principal officers of the executive departments or of such other body as Congress may by law provide, transmit to the ***Chancellor*** Pro Tempore of the Senate and the Speaker of the House of Representatives their written declaration that the President is unable to discharge the powers and duties of his office, the ***Chancellor*** shall immediately assume the powers and duties of the office as Acting President.
d) Thereafter, when the President transmits to the ***Chancellor*** Pro Tempore of the Senate and the Speaker of the House of Representatives his written declaration that no inability exists, he shall resume the powers and duties of his office unless the ***Chancellor*** and a majority of either the principal officers of the executive departments or of such other body as Congress may by law provide, transmit within four days to the ***Chancellor*** Pro Tempore of the Senate and the Speaker of the House of Representatives their written declaration that the President is unable to discharge the powers and duties of his office. Thereupon Congress shall decide the issue, assembling within forty eight hours for that purpose if not in session. If the Congress, within twenty one days after receipt of the latter written declaration, or, if Congress is not in

session, within twenty one days after Congress is required to assemble, determines by two-thirds vote of both chambers that the President is unable to discharge the powers and duties of his office, the ***Chancellor*** shall continue to discharge the same as Acting President; otherwise, the President shall resume the powers and duties of his office.

1.6 Compensation: The President shall, at stated times, receive for their services, a compensation, which shall neither be increased nor diminished during the period for which they shall have been elected, and they shall not receive within that period any other emolument from the United States, or any of them, ***or from any other foreign or domestic entity or individual.***

COMMENTARY: The President's only compensation while in office must come from the US Treasury.

1.7 Oath of Office Before the President enters on the execution of his office, he shall take the following oath or affirmation:

"I do solemnly swear (or affirm) that I will faithfully execute the office of President of the United States, and will to the best of my ability, preserve, protect and defend Constitution II of the United States."

Section 2 - Civilian Power over Military; the Cabinet, Pardon Power, and Appointments

The President shall be Commander in Chief of the Armed Forces of the United States, and of the militia of the several states, when called into the actual service of the United States; he may require the opinion, in writing, of the principal officer in each of the executive departments, upon any subject relating to the duties of their respective offices, and he shall have power to grant reprieves and pardons for offenses against the United States, except in cases of impeachment.

As Commander in Chief, the President may order the use of military force in a war properly declared by Congress. In the absence of a declaration of war, the President may employ military force to defend the United States or its allies, provided that the President notifies Congress within 48 hours of the beginning of such a military operation, and provided also that Congress issues an AUMF (Authorized Use of Military Force) for this specific military operation within 7 days after such a military operation commences. The President shall not use the military for any operation within the United States unless Congress specifically authorizes such use.

COMMENTARY: This provision codifies the Authorized Use of Military Force doctrine within Constitution II as well as the Posse Comitatus Act of 1878, which made it illegal for the President to use the military for domestic purposes.

He shall have Power, by and with the advice and consent of the Senate, to make treaties; and he shall nominate, and by and with the advice and consent of the Senate, shall appoint ambassadors, other public ministers and consuls, and all other officers of the Executive Branch, whose appointments are not herein otherwise provided for, and which shall be established by law: but Congress may by law vest the appointment of such inferior officers, as they think proper, in the President alone, in the courts of law, or in the heads of departments.

In all cases of Presidential nominations, if the Senate fails to approve or disapprove a nomination within 60 calendar days after the President has made the nomination, the President may appoint the nominee without Senate action.

COMMENTARY: This provision allows the President to staff Executive Departments without undue delays from Congress.

Every Executive Branch position requiring Senate confirmation must also have a deputy position filled by a civil servant, who shall assume the duties of the Presidentially appointed position whenever that position becomes vacant.

COMMENTARY: This new provision prevents a President from stacking the deck with presidential appointees in defiance of the wishes of Congress. Having a civil service deputy for every political appointee (a practice followed by Great Britain) also greatly assists with a smooth transition between administrations.

Section 3 - State of the Union, Convening Congress, ***and Executive Orders***

COMMENTARY: Executive Orders (EO's) are nowhere mentioned in the 1787 Constitution. Historically, presidents have used them to get around Congress and to expand the "imperial presidency". This new section recognizes that an EO may sometimes be needed, but it allows Congress to block it.

The President shall from time to time give to the Congress information on the state of the Union, and recommend for their consideration such measures as he shall judge necessary and expedient; he may, on extraordinary occasions, convene both chambers, or either of them, and in case of disagreement between them with respect to the time of adjournment, he may adjourn them to such time as he shall think proper; he shall receive ambassadors and other public ministers; he shall take care that the laws be faithfully executed, and shall commission all the officers of the United States.

In carrying out his responsibility to "take care that the laws be faithfully executed", the President may issue edicts (often called "Executive Orders" or other synonym) which have the same effect as the law upon which the Executive Order is based, provided that

- ***The Executive Order specifies the law or Constitutional provision which gives the President the authority to issue the order,***
- ***any Executive Order will have an effective date not less than thirty days from its issuance (not counting days during which Congress is not in session),***
- ***either chamber by majority vote taken during that 30-day waiting period may prevent an Executive Order from coming into effect, and***
- ***Congress may waive, shorten, or extend the waiting period at any time during the waiting period.***

Section 4 - Disqualification

The President and all civil officers of the United States shall be removed from office ***and disqualified from further public service*** on Impeachment for, and conviction of, treason, bribery, or other high crimes and misdemeanors. ***The President and all civil officers of the United States can be impeached even after leaving office.***

COMMENTARY: During trump's second impeachment trial, Trump's defenders advanced the argument that this impeachment trial was both irrelevant and ineffective, since Trump himself was already out of office and therefore could not be removed. But think now on the effect, had he been convicted. In that case, and in accordance with the 1787 Constitution, the Senate would have then voted on the question of Trump's disqualification to run for President again. This new provision in Constitution II makes disqualification automatic if the impeached official is convicted.

The President and subordinate officers have no immunity from prosecution due to their high office. They can be held accountable for abuse of power, failure to perform their official duties, and unconstitutional acts, in addition to violations of criminal and civil law.

COMMENTARY: This new provision insures that the President and other officers have no immunity from prosecution due to their occupying a high office.

Article III: The Judicial Branch

Section 1 – Federal Courts

1.1 The judicial power of the United States shall be vested in one Supreme Court ***and one Constitutional Court*** and in such appellate and district courts as the Congress may from time to time ordain and establish.

COMMENTARY: The Constitutional Court is a new feature of Constitution II. Its purpose is to provide rapid judicial review of Executive Branch and Legislative Branch actions.

1.2 The Chancellor of the Senate has the power to nominate and appoint all Federal judges with the advice and consent of the Seante.

COMMENTARY: The Chancellor rather than the President makes all judicial appointments. All judicial appointments require Senate confirmation by majority vote. (This change is a major component in curbing the Imperial Presidency.)

1.3 ***All judges shall serve a 16-year term of office;*** and shall, at stated times, receive for their services a compensation which shall not be diminished during their continuance in office.

COMMENTARY: A term of office for the Federal judiciary is a new feature of Constitution II. The purpose is to make judges a bit more accountable.

1.4 Eligibility. All judicial nominees must hold a law degree from an accredited law school and must be a member of the bar in good standing in a jurisdiction within the United States. Congress may waive the eligibility requirements for a particular nominee.

COMMENTARY: Eligibility standards for Federal judges are a new feature of Constitution II. The purpose is to ensure that Federal judges have some legal training and experience, and to prevent the appointment of people who are merely favorites of the Chancellor. However, this provision allows Congress to make an exception, when, for example, a Chancellor wished to nominate a self-trained legal expert.

1.5 Composition of the courts.

1.5.1 Chief Justice of the United States. When the office of Chief Justice of the United States becomes vacant, the sitting Associate Justices of the Supreme and Constitutional Courts shall appoint a new Chief Justice from among their own number. The Chief Justice shall serve a 16-year term of office and shall preside over both the Supreme Court and the Constitutional Court.

COMMENTARY: The method of selecting a new Chief Justice is a new feature of Constitution II. It adds both stability and continuity to the courts, and it encourages collegiality among justices.

1.5.2 Supreme Court. In addition to the Chief Justice, the Supreme Court shall consist of eight Associate Justices.

1.5.3 Constitutional Court. In addition to the Chief Justice, the Constitutional Court shall consist of eight Associate Justices.

Section 2 – Judicial Power, Judicial Review, Original Jurisdiction, and Jury Trials

2.1 Judicial Power. The judicial power of Federal courts shall extend to all cases, in law and equity, arising under Constitution II, the laws of the United States, and treaties and international laws recognized by the United States; controversies involving ministers of foreign states, between two or more states, between a state and citizens of another state, between citizens of different states, and between a state or its citizens and foreign states or citizens ; and all controversies to which the United States shall be a party

2.2 Judicial Review: Original Jurisdiction of the Constitutional Court . The Constitutional Court shall review acts of the Legislative Branch and shall have the power to invalidate any law, or any part of any law, found by the court not to be in compliance with Constitution II. The Constitutional Court shall also review all acts of the Executive Branch and shall have the power to invalidate any such acts, found by the court not to be in compliance with Constitution II or the laws of the United States. In conducting judicial reviews of both the Legislative and the Executive branches, the Constitutional Court may consider both the inscribed provisions of Constitution II and laws enacted by Congress, as well as their intent. Any member of Congress may initiate a judicial review by the Constitutional Court, and said review must be completed within 90 days of the referral from Congress.

COMMENTARY: The Constitutional Court insures that judicial review of any law or executive action is available, and the fact that any member of Congress may initiate a judicial review insures that it is available quickly.

2.3 Original Jurisdiction of the Supreme Court. In all cases affecting ambassadors, other public ministers and consuls, and those in which a state shall be party, the Supreme Court shall have original jurisdiction. In all the other cases before mentioned, ***excepting judicial review cases under the jurisdiction of the***

Constitutional Court, the Supreme Court shall have appellate jurisdiction, both as to law and fact, with such exceptions, and under such regulations as Congress shall make.

2.4 Jury Trials. The trial of all crimes, except in cases of Impeachment, shall be by jury; and such trial shall be held in the state where the said crimes shall have been committed; but when not committed within any state, the trial shall be at such place or places as the Congress may by law have directed.

Section 3 - Treason

Treason against the United States shall consist only in levying war against the United States, or in adhering to the enemies of the United States, giving them aid and comfort. No person shall be convicted of treason unless on the testimony of two witnesses to the same overt act, or on confession in open court.

The punishment for treason is death.

Article IV: Debts, Supremacy, and Oaths

COMMENTARY: With the exception of the paragraph concerning the so-called "national debt ceiling", Article IV copies analogous provisions from the 1787 Constitution, which guaranteed continuity with the preceding Articles of Confederation.

All debts contracted and engagements entered into before the adoption of ***Constitution II*** shall be as valid against the United States under ***Constitution II*** as under the 1787 Constitution.

All existing laws, treaties, regulations, and debts, of the United States, undertaken under the Constitution of 1787 as amended, continue in full force and effect, except where specifically altered by Constitution II.

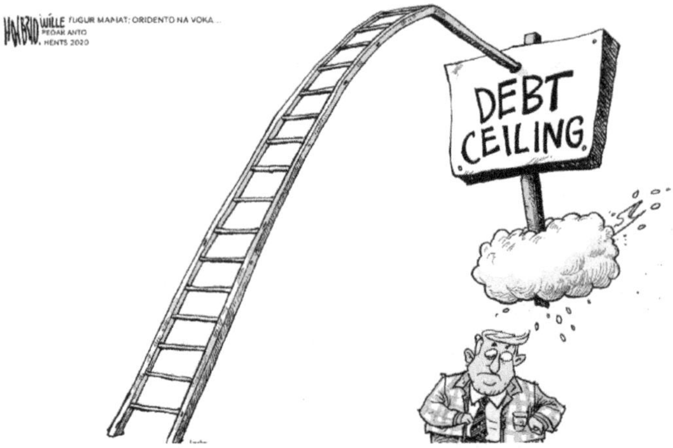

The "National Debt Ceiling" is a fiction

The notion of a "national debt ceiling" has no meaning. When the United States Treasury borrows money to fund expenditures authorized by Congress, then those debts are a sovereign debt of this nation and must be repaid.

COMMENTARY: This provision dispenses with arguments about whether this nation will agree to pay its bills.

Constitution II, and the Laws of the United States which shall be made in pursuance thereof; and all treaties made, or which shall be made, under the authority of the United States, shall be the supreme law of the land; and the judges in every state shall be bound thereby, anything in Constitution II or laws of any state to the contrary notwithstanding.

The Senators and Representatives before mentioned, and the members of the several state legislatures, and all executive and judicial officers, both of the United States and of the several states, shall be bound by oath or affirmation, to support Constitution II; but no religious test ***or test of loyalty to a person or a political party*** shall ever be required as a qualification to any office or public trust under the United States.

COMMENTARY:In the trump Administration, aA test of political or personal loyalty appears to be required for any public official to continue in office, even if the official is a civil servant. All such tests must be made unconstitutional.

Article V: Elections

COMMENTARY: Article V is all new.

Section 1. General Provisions

1.1 The Franchise

All American citizens who have attained the age of 18 are entitled and required to vote in every Federal election. Failure to vote may be sanctioned, as directed by Congress.

COMMENTARY: Voting is compulsory, as it is in 22 nations around the globe, whose populations total 744 million people. The argument in favor of universal compulsory voting is obvious: Such a constitutional provision prevents any politician from restricting the franchise to a favored subset of the population. Penalizing those who fail to vote is not mandatory; rather, penalizing politicians who try to prevent people from voting is the real point.

Democracy works best when everyone shows up.

Location: Every voter votes in the state and election district in which they reside. American citizens who do not reside in any state vote in the Non-State Election District, which consists of US territories and possessions plus lands outside the United States.

Making Democracy official -- one voter at a time

State Voter Registration

State Voter Registration Responsibility: Every state shall

- ***automatically register each citizen to vote upon their 18th birthday or whenever a citizen over age 18 interacts with the state or a Federal government entity,***
- ***maintain for each voter both their legal (voting) address and current contact information,***
- ***annotate the voter record to indicate a voter who has deceased or moved out of state, and***
- ***establish appropriate means of voter authentication.***

1.2 Conduct of elections

All elections are conducted by the several states. The Secretary of State conducts elections for the Non-State Election District. A secret ballot is guaranteed. All votes must be received by election day. Voters may cast their ballots (1) by mail, (2) in person for one week ending on election day, or (3) online (if security can be assured); except that any state may choose to conduct its entire election by mail.

COMMENTARY: The current practice of counting votes which arrive after polls are closed simply encourages people to wait until the last minute to vote and then delays the final vote count while everyone is waiting for the final results to be announced. Far better to tell everyone to get their votes in well before the deadline to insure that their votes will be counted. In this way, final results can be tabulated and announced hours (rather than days) after the polls close.

All Federal elections (for President, Chancellor, Senate, and House) have a single winner. A primary election narrows the field to three candidates for the general election, which determines the winner.

1.3 Ranked Choice Voting

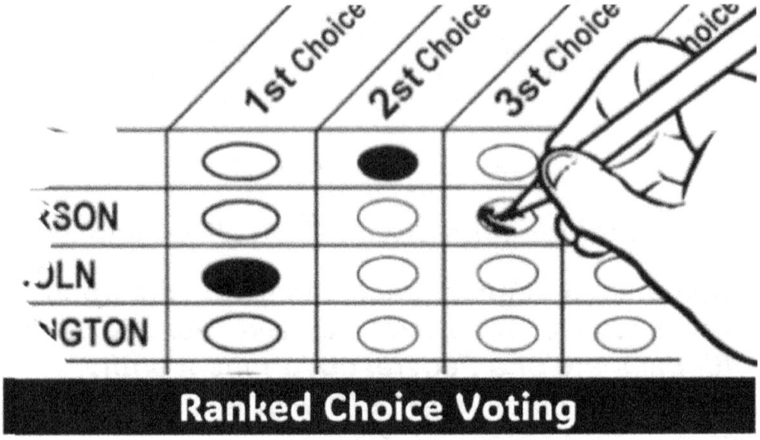

Ranked Choice Voting (RCV) is mandatory for all Federal elections. The United States will employ the following Ranked Choice Voting procedure

---

COMMENTARY: Many RCV procedures exist, and some are quite complex. This is one of the simplest.

- ***After selecting their 1st choice for any office, voters are allowed to also select a 2nd and, if desired, a 3rd choice.***
- ***When counting ballots, only the 1st choice votes are counted. The candidate with the fewest 1st choice votes is eliminated, and ballots cast for that candidate are reassigned to the voter's 2nd and then 3rd choice. If the ballot has no choice remaining for a surviving candidate, then that ballot is exhausted.***
    - ***Primary Election: This process continues until three candidates remain. These are the only***

candidates whose names will appear on the general election ballot.

COMMENTARY: Of course, in both the primary and the general election, voters will still be able to write in a candidate not on the ballot.

- ***General Election: This process continues until one candidate, the winner, remains.***

1.4 Open primaries

COMMENTARY: Open primaries do not eliminate the role of political parties. Parties can still endorse candidates, raise money, and campaign for candidates and issues. Open primaries allow every voter to select their favored candidates for each office, regardless of the party of either the voter or the candidate.

Open primaries are mandatory for all Federal elections. Open primaries are open to all candidates whether or not affiliated with a political party; the party affiliation of a candidate, if any, can be indicated on the ballot if the candidate so chooses. All registered voters are required to vote in every primary and general election within the jurisdiction of their voting residence.

Any eligible candidate may compete in any open primary, subject to state rules for qualifying for the ballot. The results

of the primaries determine the candidates whose names will appear on the general election ballot. Those eligible to compete in the general election may withdraw within one week after the primary results are known.

Any American citizen who meets the eligibility criteria for an elected office may become a candidate for that office, with these provisos:

- ***No one can be a candidate for more than one Federal or state office at a time.***
- ***No one may be a candidate who participated in, contributed to, or in any way gave material support to any insurrection against the United States, including the insurrection from 1861 to 1865, the January 6, 2021 insurrection, and any other which may occur in future. This includes any member of Congress who voted to not accept the Electoral College vote on January 6 and any who voted not to impeach Trump for his attempted coup. Any Federal or state level officials, whether elected or appointed, who supported Donald Trump's attempted coup are likewise disqualified from further service to the United States or any state. (Important note: Other than disqualification to serve in the future, Trump and his supporters must not be prosecuted for their role in the attempted coup.) Congress, by a two-thirds vote in both chambers, can remove this disqualification for a particular individual.***

COMMENTARY: This disqualification clause is directed at the courts which failed to follow the 14th Amendment to the 1787 Constitution. That Amendment should have prevented insurrectionists and their sympathizers (like Trump himself) from running for office after the January 6, 2021 insurrection.

1.5 Election dates

COMPRESSED ELECTION SCHEDULE				
Congress Adjourns	Primary Election	General Election	Congress Convenes	Presidential Inauguration
July 4	September 1	November 15	December 1	December 10

All elections have a voting period of one month for mail-in ballots and one week for in-person voting. Regular primary elections for all Federal offices end on September 1. General elections end on November 15. The new Congress convenes on December 1. The new Chancellor takes office on December 1. The new President is inaugurated on December 10.

COMMENTARY: This eliminates the lame-duck session of Congress and curtails the inter-regnum between the presidential election and the Inauguration.

During the last week of each election, the 1st choice votes for each candidate will be announced daily.

COMMENTARY: Most votes will have been counted before the polls close on election day, so the final results should be made available within hours.

1.5 Fundraising and transparency

No candidate for a Federal office may personally engage in fundraising or appear at a fundraising event while Congress is in session.

COMMENTARY: We do not want elected officials campaigning for election when they should be doing their day job, that is, representing "we the people". Nor do we want people not currently elected to get a leg up on campaigning while current officeholders are forbidden to campaign. Hence, this provision precludes anyone from fundraising while Congress is in session. Since the Congressional session will end by July 4 of each election year, fundraising and campaigning by all candidates can occur thereafter.

To appear on a primary ballot, a candidate must authorize the US Treasury to release, two weeks before the primary, the five most recent tax returns of that candidate and their spouse; and the candidate must also release, on the same schedule, a statement of net worth, showing all of their assets and liabilities and those of their spouse.

Financial Disclosure

A write-in candidate in the primary who qualifies for the general election must effect the same release of tax returns and net worth within two weeks after the primary.

After the general election, and before being allowed to take office, the winner must authorize the US Treasury to release tax returns and a statement of net worth, as outlined above.

These regulations guarantee financial transparency for all candidates and election victors. If any candidate has a conflict of interest, the public has a right to know about it before the election takes place.

Section 2. Elections for President and Chancellor

2.1 Elections and Terms of Office.

The President and the Chancellor shall each be elected directly by the voters for a four-year term of office. The President shall be elected in years evenly divisible by 4. The Chancellor shall be elected in even-numbered years not evenly divisible by 4.

COMMENTARY: Separating the election of the President from the election of Number Two is a major step forward for democracy. In the current system, each Presidential candidate chooses the Vice Presidential candidate, without significant input from the public. (While we do vote for a combined ticket of President and Vice President, few voters consider the Vice Presidential candidate as determinative of their choice.) And yet on 14 occasions, the Vice President has subsequently become President, which means that the selection of the Vice Presidential candidate is enormously significant. Perhaps the selection of the second most powerful position in the nation should be made by the people, don't you think? To the contrary argument, that the President needs a partner he can work with, I would answer that a President can appoint as many advisors as they want, but these advisors do not stand in line to accede to the presidency. In addition, nothing in the 1787 Constitution requires the President to work with the Vice President at all. For example, when FDR died, he had met with Vice President Harry Truman exactly three times, and Truman did not even know about the Manhattan Project (the invention of the atomic bomb). Several vice presidents have quipped that the Vice President's only real job is to inquire every day at the White House as to the President's health. So let's turn the Vice President of the United States into the Chancellor of the Senate and also give them a real job to do, namely, making all judicial appointments.

2.2 Vote Tabulation Committee (VTC)

Vote Tabulation Committee

Congress shall establish a Vote Tabulation Committee, whose responsibility is to apply the Ranked Choice Voting procedures on a national basis in the primary and general elections for President and for Chancellor. The VTC will collect from the states the number of first choice votes for each candidate, tabulate and summarize the results, eliminate the candidate with the fewest votes after each round of counting, and announce the winners.

COMMENTARY: The task of counting votes for President or Chancellor with Ranked Choice Voting is actually quite straightforward. Each state sends its list of first choice votes to the Vote Tabulation Committee (VTC). The VTC consolidates the lists from all jurisdictions, then eliminates the candidate with the fewest votes, and instructs each state to submit a new list after having dropped the candidate who was eliminated and reassigned votes for that candidate to each voter's next highest choice.

Section 3. Elections for Congress

3.1 Census, redistricting schedule, and apportionment.

The census will be taken every decade in years ending in 0. Once each decade, in years ending in 1, the new census will be used for the purpose of apportionment and re-districting. The entire Congress will then be elected from the new districts in years ending in 2. These district boundaries will then be used in all elections until the next census.

COMMENTARY: While the 1787 Constitution mandates that a census be taken every decade, and that the census be used for apportionment of House seats among the states, redistricting within a state is not addressed directly. Supreme Court decisions have mandated districts of equal population, but have not spoken about redistricting between censuses. Article V Section 3.1 clears this up: The census will be taken at the beginning of each decade and will be used for apportionment and redistricting for the entire decade.

CONGRESSIONAL REPRESENTATION		
	1787 Constitution	Constitution II
population per House member		
...in 1787	30,000	
...in 1929	277,000	
...today	730,000	
...proposed for tomorrow		<500,000
Senators	2 per state	<1% of US population

Each state shall be apportioned a number of seats in the House of Representatives such that no Congressional District shall have a population greater than 500,000, but each state shall have at least one Representative. Each state will be subdivided into Congressional Districts of equal population.

COMMENTARY: This will greatly increase the size of the House and make it more representative of the people, to wit, a maximum of 500k people per member rather than the average 730k at present. The new House will have approximately 700 members.

Each state shall be apportioned a number of seats in the Senate such that every Senatorial District shall have a population greater than 1% of the US population, but every state shall have at least one Senator. Each state will be subdivided into Senatorial Districts of equal population.

COMMENTARY: The U.S. Senate may be the most anti-democratic institution created by the 1787 Constitution. With two Senators per state, the larger states are seriously underrepresented, and the smallest states are overrepresented. In 1787 the most lopsided ratio (Virginia to Delaware) was 13 to 1 – that is, a Senator from Virginia represented 13 times as many people as a Senator from Delaware. Today the worst ratio is 69 to 1 (California to Wyoming). If you live in Wyoming and come to Washington to see your Senator, you have a reasonably good shot at getting in the door, since each of your Senators represents on average 288,000 people (half of Wyoming's 2020 population). But if you come from California, you better be a mega-donor or other bigwig to meet with your Senator, because you must compete with an average of 19,769,000 Californians per Senator. The current system is totally unreasonable, and the only solution is to reconstitute the Senate as a proportionally representative body.

In the new Senate, 35 states (including DC and Puerto Rico) will have 1 Senator, and 17 will have multiple. The Senate membership will be about 100, as at present.

The Non-State Election District shall elect one Senator and one Representative.

COMMENTARY: People who do not reside in any state fall into several buckets. Residents of Washington, DC can vote for President but have no representation in Congress. People who moved overseas but used to live in a state can vote in that state, even though they no longer live there. People who reside in a US territory or possession (Puerto Rico, Guam, US Virgin Islands) have no vote at all. This ridiculous hodge podge is fixed by Constitution II" DC and Puerto Rico can become states if they choose to do so. All citizens of US territories and possessions and all other overseas American citizens live in the Non-State Election District (NS) and elect one member of each chamber in Congress. Thus expats will have a voice, and all citizens get to vote for President and Chancellor.

3.2 Composition of the Senate

Seats in the Senate shall be divided as equally as they may be into two classes (Class I and Class II). For any state, the number of seats assigned to each Class shall be the same, as nearly as possible. Class I seats will be elected for a six-year term in years ending in 2, and for a four-year term in years ending in 8. Class II seats will be elected for a four-year term in years ending in 2, and for a six-year term in years ending in 6.

COMMENTARY: Thus the whole Senate will be elected in years ending in 2, half of the Senate in years ending in 6, and half in years ending in 8. The basic idea here is to retain the notion of longer terms and a measure of continuity in the Senate as compared to the House, but also to provide for the election of the entire Senate following the decennial census when Senatorial districts will be altered.

3.3 Drawing election district boundaries

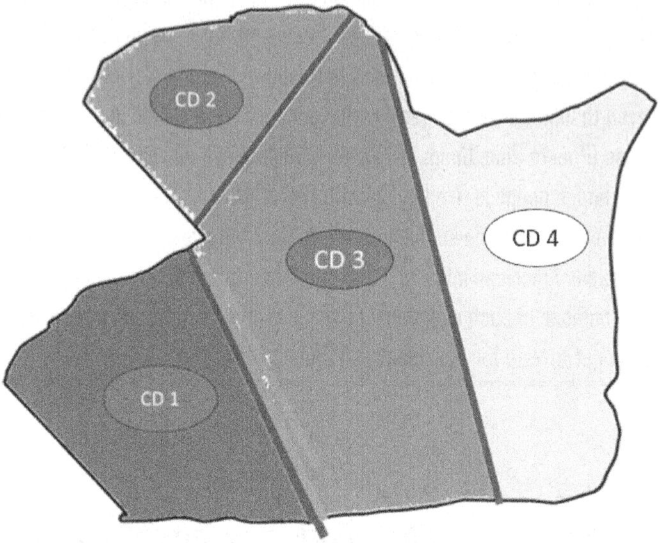

Completed CD boundaries for an imaginary state

For all legislative districts, including the US Senate, US House of Representatives, and state legislatures, the only permissible criteria for drawing election district boundaries are equalizing the population among districts within a state and geographic proximity. The following procedure must be used, unless modified or refined by Congress:

COMMENTARY: Many schemes can be devised that satisfy the twin criteria of equal population in each district and geographic proximity. This is one such scheme, which has the advantage of simplicity and ease of replication. Appendix I contains an abbreviated example of the application of this scheme to an imaginary state.

Calculate the target population of each election district. Then repeat these steps to draw each district:

1. ***On a map of the state, draw a straight line connecting the most widely separated points within that portion of the state not yet assigned to an election district. This is the Reference Line. Note: If two or more potential reference lines are of the same length, the following rules will be applied in order to break the tie:***

a. Select as the Reference Line the potential reference line whose westernmost point is farthest to the west.

b. Select as the Reference Line the potential reference line whose westernmost point is farthest to the north.

c. Select as the Reference Line the potential reference line whose easternmost point is farthest to the north.

2. ***Select the westernmost point on the Reference Line as the Starting Point.***
3. ***Draw a line perpendicular to the Reference Line and through the Starting Point. This is the Drag Line.***
4. ***Drag the Drag Line away from the Starting Point, keeping it perpendicular to the Reference Line. As the Drag Line moves away from the Starting Point, add population and territory between the Drag Line and the Starting Point to the election district being constructed. Stop dragging when the target population has been reached.***

COMMENTARY: Appendix I provides a pictorial representation of the operation of this redistricting scheme on an imaginary state.

Section 5. Continuance in Office

To continue in office, all Federal elected officials, by October 1 of each year, must authorize the US Treasury to release the five most recent tax returns of that official and their spouse. Each official must also release, on the same schedule, a statement of net worth, showing all of their assets and liabilities and those of their spouse.

COMMENTARY: These are the same financial reporting rules as those specified earlier for candidates. Here these reporting rules are specified for annual reporting by all elected officeholders.

Federal elected officials are prohibited from hiring, nominating, or appointing any member of their immediate family to any position within the Federal Government.

COMMENTARY: The 1787 Constitution does not address nepotism, and the 1967 Ani-Nepotism Act has been interpreted as not applying to the President. Therefore, this clause is a new addition in constitution II.

Article VI: Constitutional Amendments

Section 1. Proposing an amendment

1. Congress, by law, can propose an amendment to the Constitution.

2. ***Once every 10 years, in years ending in 5, Congress must call a Constitutional Amendments Convention. Voters in each Congressional District shall elect one Delegate to this convention. A Delegate must be a registered voter residing within the CD, who is neither an elected public official nor an officer of any political party. This convention may propose amendments to the Constitution.***

COMMENTARY: The amendment process specified in the 1787 Constitution fails the democracy test as to both elements: 1) proposing an amendment and 2) ratifying a proposed amendment. Constitution II addresses both of these deficiencies. As to proposing amendments, the procedure specified here for a decennial Constitutional Amendments Convention is modeled on a similar device used by the State of Florida to propose amendments to that state's constitution. The ratification problem is addressed by Article VI Section 2.

Section 2. Ratifying a proposed amendment

Amendments Ratified

1. ***Proposed amendments will appear on the ballot at the next general election.***
2. ***If fewer than half the voters approve, then the amendment is defeated.***
3. ***If 60% of the voters approve, then the amendment is ratified.***
4. ***If a majority, but less than 60%, approve, then the proposed amendment will appear for a second time at the next subsequent general election.***
    a. ***If 60% approve on this second attempt, then the amendment is ratified.***
    b. ***If a majority of all voters approve, and if a majority of voters in states that contain 60% of the US population approve, then the amendment is ratified.***

Democracy Recaptured

APPENDIX 1. APPLICATION OF PROPOSED REDISTRICTING SCHEME TO AN IMAGINARY STATE

The drawings in this appendix display the proposed redistricting scheme applied to an imaginary state.

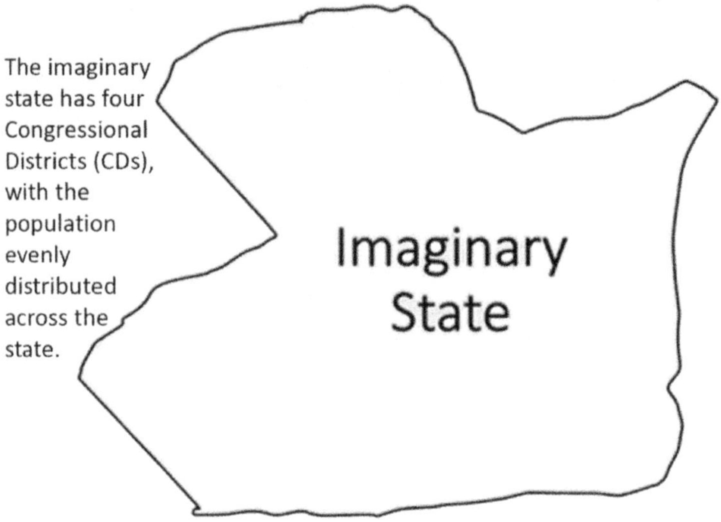

An Imaginary State with 4 CDs

Repeat these steps to draw each CD:

1. On a map of the state, draw a straight line connecting the most widely separated points within that portion of the state not yet assigned to an election district. This is the Reference Line.

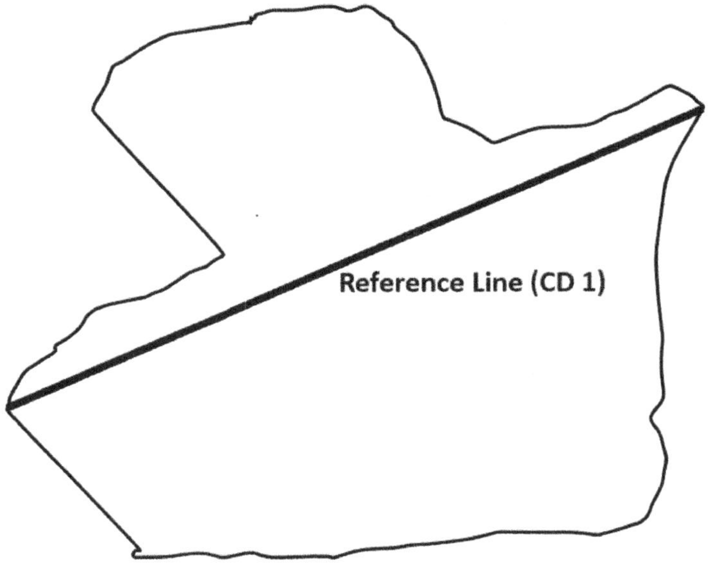

Sometimes two potential reference lines of the same length will appear. This is the procedure for handling that situation:

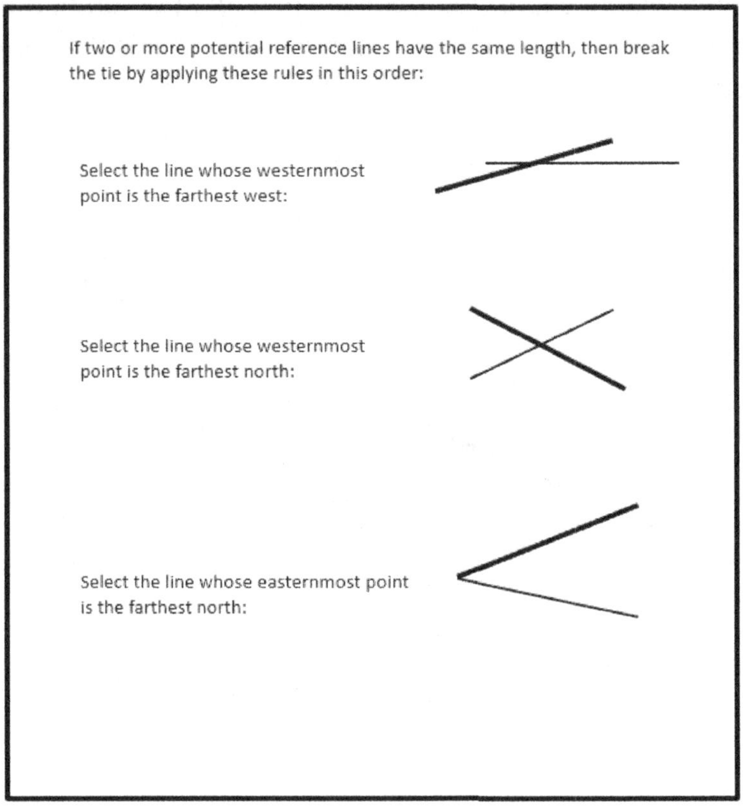

Breaking a tie if two potential reference lines are of equal length

2. Select the westernmost point on the Reference Line as the Starting Point.

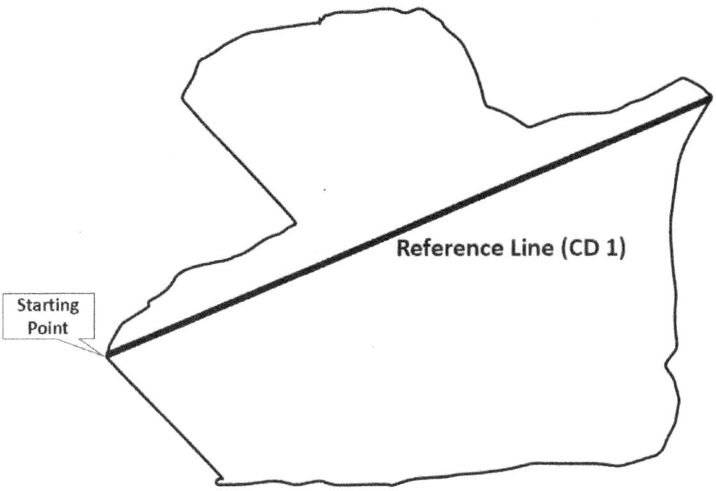

Marking the Starting Point for CD 1

3. Draw a line perpendicular to the Reference Line and through the Starting Point. This is the Drag Line.

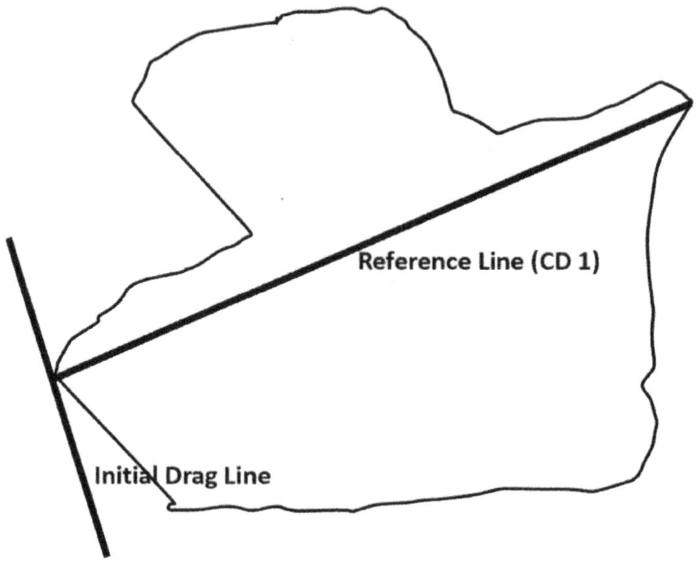

4. Drag the Drag Line away from the Starting Point, keeping it perpendicular to the Reference Line. As the Drag Line moves away from the Starting Point, add population and territory between the starting Point and the Drag Line to the election district being constructed.

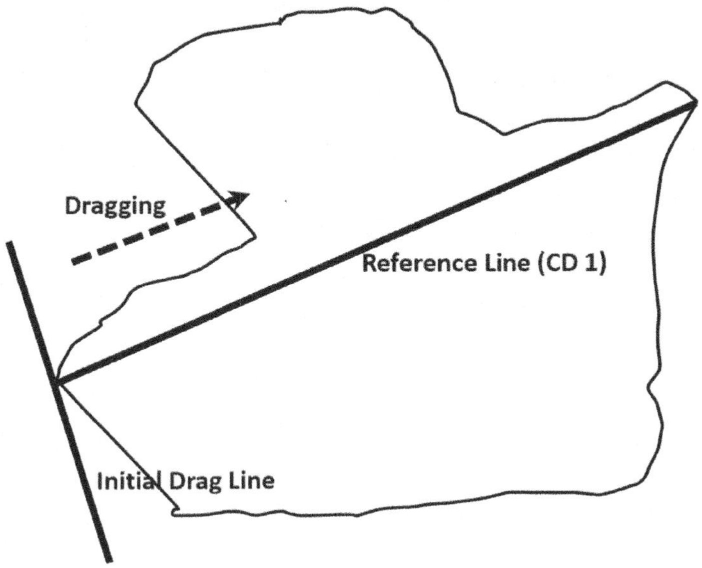

Stop dragging when the target population has been reached.

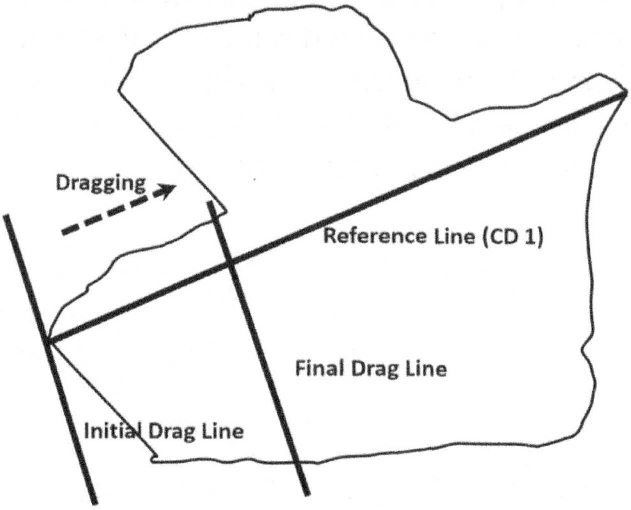

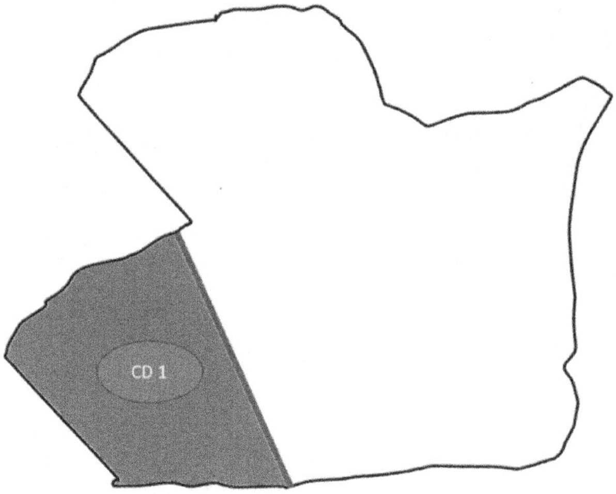

Now repeat these steps to construct CD 2.

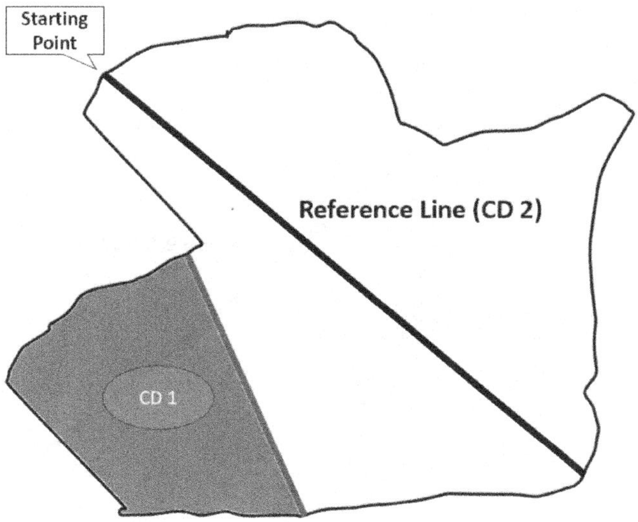

Drawing the Reference Line and selecting the Starting Point for CD 2

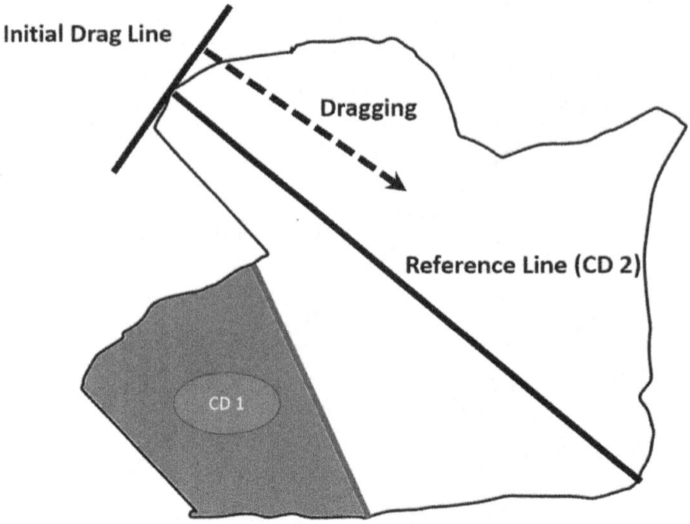
Initial Drag Line
Dragging
Reference Line (CD 2)
CD 1

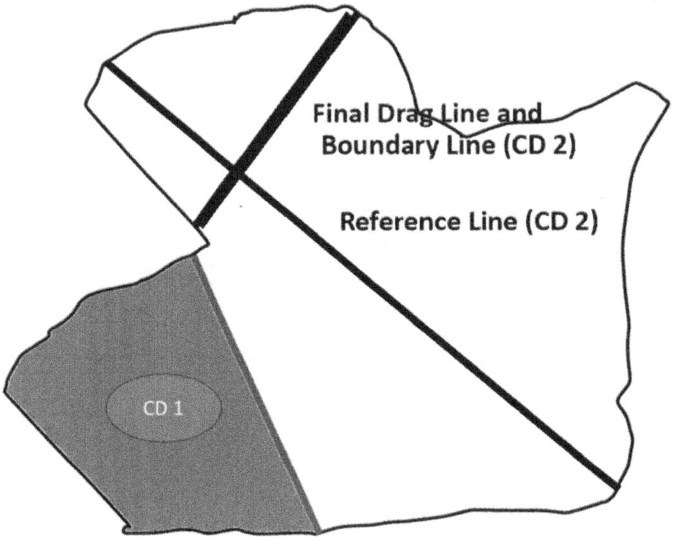
Final Drag Line and
Boundary Line (CD 2)
Reference Line (CD 2)
CD 1

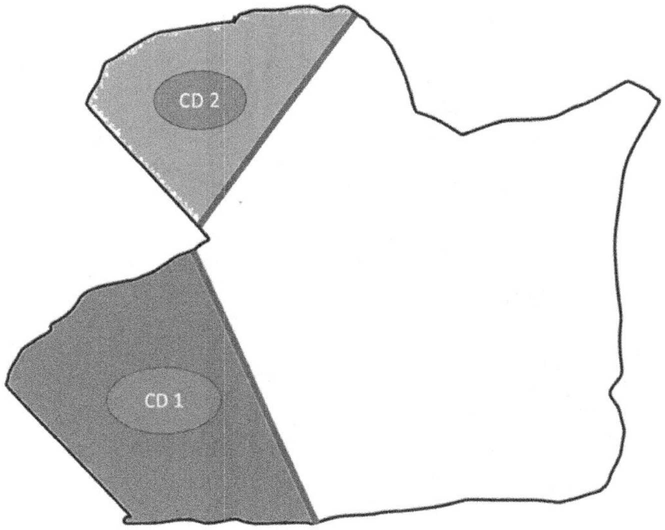

Filling in the completed CD 2

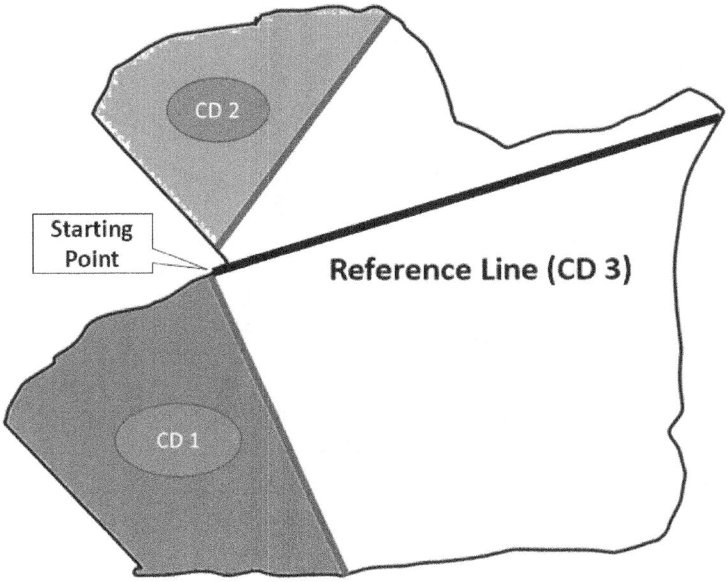

Drawing the Reference Line and Starting Point for CD 3

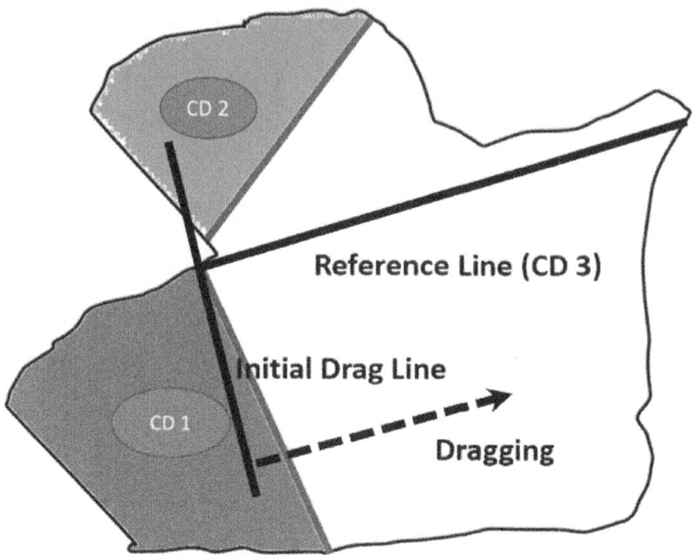
CD 2
CD 1
Reference Line (CD 3)
Initial Drag Line
Dragging

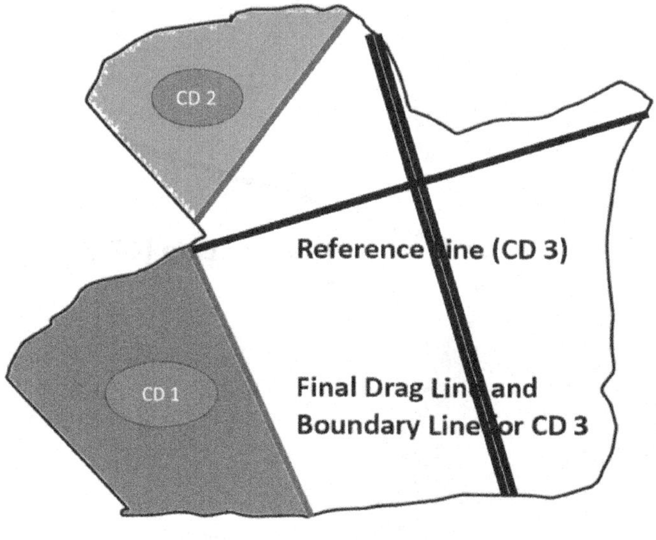
CD 2
CD 1
Reference Line (CD 3)
Final Drag Line and
Boundary Line for CD 3

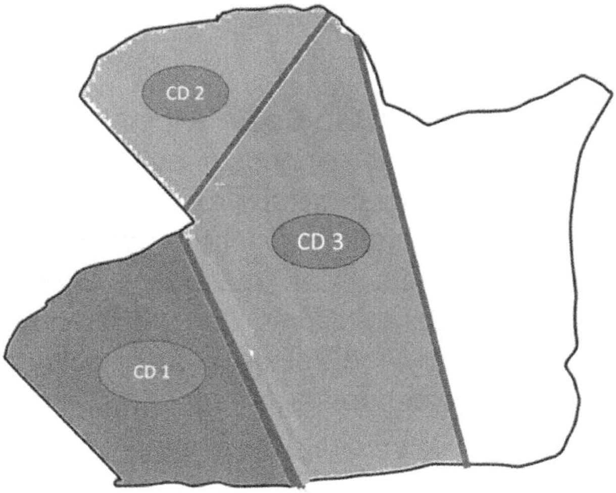

When all district boundaries have been drawn except for the last one, one need not draw any more boundaries, since by definition the last district will contain all of the territory and population not already part of another district:

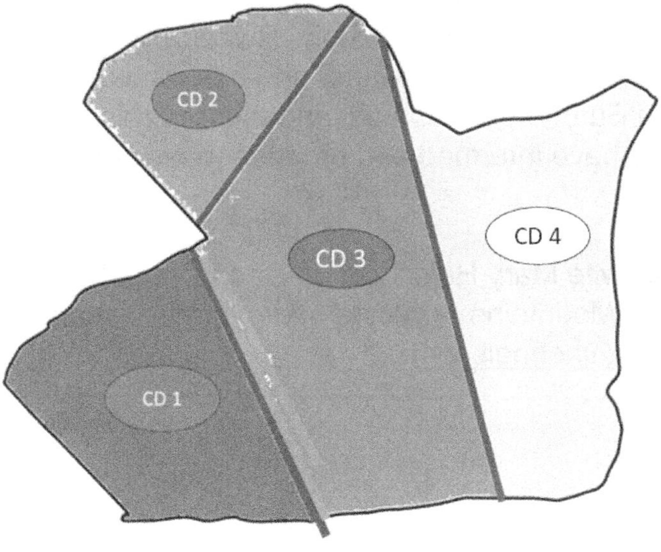

All CDs completed for the Imaginary State

About the Author, Dr. Bob Spear

Wild Ride to Democracy is **Bob Spear's** third book of political commentary, but the first that responds directly and forcefully to Donald Trump's assault on democracy. Dr. Spear is an active Democrat, the Democratic candidate for the Maryland House of Delegates in 2022, and the current Treasurer of the Garrett County (Maryland) Democratic Central Committee. He is one of the founders of Mountain Maryland Voices, a grassroots organization in Western Maryland dedicated to saving our democracy from autocracy.

A retired computer professor from Prince George's Community College, Maryland, Dr. Spear was Executive Director and then Senior Advisor to National CyberWatch Center. He has authored and published many books and technical papers in computer programming, instructional technology, distance learning, and cybersecurity.

A world traveler always interested in political systems around the globe, Bob has lived in Austria and Iran, has worked on projects in Poland, Denmark, Norway, Ethiopia, Rwanda, South Africa, Ghana, Tanzania, Zambia, and Botswana, and has visited dozens of other countries in Europe, Africa, Asia, and the Americas. These experiences have informed and broadened his political and cultural perspective.

Bob and his wife Mary Helen live on Deep Creek Lake in the Appalachian Mountains of Western Maryland. He can be reached at bob_spear@hotmail.com.

.

Made in the USA
Coppell, TX
12 June 2026

81393197R00077